kids cook!

3-in-1
Cookbook Collection

Bag Lunches
After-School Snacks
Weekend Treats

Jean Paré

Welcome

Attention, aspiring chefs! You'll find fun recipes in our new *Kids Cook! 3-in-1 Cookbook Collection*, a fantastic combination of three books in one, just for you. Follow the easy step-by-step instructions and colourful pictures to create just the right school lunch, after-school snack, or special treat for you.

Wish you could plan and make your own lunch? You can, with the mix-and-match recipes in *Bag Lunches*—from sandwiches and wraps to yummy salads and sweet desserts.

Summertime Snack Mix, page 53

Need a satisfying snack after school? The ideas in *After-School Snacks* won't disappoint you. Whether it's something sweet or nutritious, or deliciously both, we have what you crave.

Want to enjoy the weekend by making a special treat? There are plenty of possibilities in *Weekend Treats*. You'll find something gooey or chocolaty, soft or crumbly, tart or tangy to share with your friends and family.

Just starting to cook? The convenient Get Ready section of each recipe lists exactly what you'll need before you start. The picture dictionary of Equipment and Utensils, on pages 6 and 7, shows what the cooking tools look like, and the Glossary Of Cooking Terms, on page 4, explains words you may have questions about. We want you to feel comfortable and be able to cook safely, so read through the Safety information on page 8. And remember: pick your recipe; get all the ingredients and equipment ready; and then get set to cook—successfully!

Table of Contents

Pickly Pita Pockets, page 29

Left: Turtle Chocolates, page 130
Right: Marshmallow Delights, page 131

Cooking Terms

Bake
To cook in an oven preheated to the temperature it says in the recipe. Use either the bottom or centre rack.

Batter
A mixture of flour, liquid and other ingredients that can be thin (such as pancake batter) or thick (such as muffin batter).

Beat
To mix two or more ingredients with a spoon, fork or electric mixer, using a circular motion.

Blend
To mix two or more ingredients with a food processor or blender until combined.

Boil
To heat a liquid in a saucepan until bubbles rise in a steady pattern and break on the surface. Steam also starts to rise from the surface.

Break An Egg
Tap the side of an egg on the edge of a bowl or cup to crack the shell. Place the tips of both thumbs in the crack and open the shell, letting the egg yolk and egg white drop into the bowl.

Broil
To cook under the top heating element in the oven. Use either the top rack or the upper rack.

Chill
To place in the refrigerator until cold.

Chop
To cut food into small pieces with a sharp knife on a cutting board; to chop finely is to cut foods as small as you can.

Combine
To put two or more ingredients together.

Cream
To beat an ingredient or combination of ingredients until the mixture is soft, smooth and "creamy," using a spoon or electric mixer.

Cut In
To combine butter or margarine with dry ingredients (such as flour) using a fork or pastry blender until the mixture looks like big crumbs the size of green peas.

Dice
To cut food into small ¼ inch (6 mm) cube-shaped pieces.

Drain
To strain away an unwanted liquid (such as water, fruit juice or grease) using a colander or strainer. Drain water or juice over the kitchen sink or in a bowl. Drain grease into a metal can, chill until hardened, then throw away in the garbage.

Drizzle
To dribble drops or lines of glaze or icing over food in a random manner from tines of a fork or the tip of a spoon.

Fold
To mix gently, using a rubber spatula, by cutting down in the centre and lifting towards the edge of the bowl. Use a "down, up, over" movement, turning the bowl as you repeat.

Garnish
To decorate food with edible condiments such as parsley sprigs, fruit slices or vegetable cut-outs.

Heat
To make something warm or hot by placing the saucepan on the stove burner that is turned on to the level it says in the recipe.

Knead
To work dough into a smooth putty-like mass by pressing and folding using the heels of your hands.

Let Stand
To let a baked product cool slightly on a wire rack or hot pad, while still in its baking pan. Also, any other mixture that requires time to sit on the counter for the flavours to blend.

Mash
To squash cooked or very ripe foods with a fork or potato masher.

Melt
To heat a solid food (such as butter, margarine, cheese or chocolate) until it turns into a liquid. Be careful not to burn it.

Mix
(see Combine)

Mixing Just Until Moistened
To stir dry ingredients with liquid ingredients until dry ingredients are barely wet. Mixture will still be lumpy.

Process
To mix or cut up food in a blender (or food processor) until it is the way it says in the recipe.

Sauté
To cook food quickly in a small amount of oil in a frying pan, wok, or special sauté pan over medium heat.

Scramble-Fry
To brown ground meat in hot oil using a spoon, fork or pancake lifter to break up the meat into small crumb-like pieces as it cooks.

Scrape (Scraping down the sides)
To use a rubber spatula to remove as much of a mixture as possible from inside a bowl or saucepan.

Simmer
To heat liquids in a saucepan on low on the stove burner so that small bubbles appear on the surface around the sides of the liquid.

Slice
To cut foods such as apples, carrots, tomatoes, meat or bread into thin sections or pieces, using a sharp knife.

Spoon (into)
Using a spoon to scoop ingredients from one container to another.

Spread
To cover the surface of one product (generally a more solid food such as bread) with another product (generally a softer food such as icing or butter).

Stir
To mix two or more ingredients with a spoon, using a circular motion.

Stir-Fry
To heat food quickly in a frying pan on medium-high, stirring constantly.

Toast
To brown slightly in a toaster or frying pan, or under the broiler in the oven.

Toss
To mix salad or other ingredients gently with a lifting motion, using two forks, two spoons or salad tongs.

Equipment & Utensils

Barbecue fork

Bread knife

Blender

Baking sheet

Colander

Casserole dish

Cookie sheet

Frying pan

Cutting board

Dry measures

Hot pad

Electric mixer

Electric frying pan

Ice-cream scoop

Mixing spoons

Measuring spoons

Loaf pan

Liquid measures

Muffin pan

Bowls (mixing)

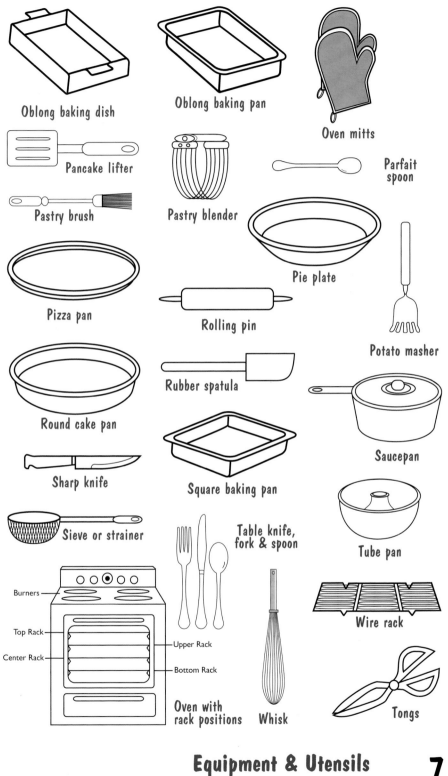

Oblong baking dish

Oblong baking pan

Oven mitts

Pancake lifter

Pastry brush

Pastry blender

Parfait spoon

Pie plate

Pizza pan

Rolling pin

Potato masher

Round cake pan

Rubber spatula

Saucepan

Sharp knife

Square baking pan

Sieve or strainer

Table knife, fork & spoon

Tube pan

Burners

Top Rack

Center Rack

Upper Rack

Bottom Rack

Oven with rack positions

Whisk

Wire rack

Tongs

Equipment & Utensils

7

Safety

Remember these safety tips to keep you cooking:

1. Never touch anything electrical with wet hands.
2. Hold on to the plug when you pull out a cord; don't pull on the cord itself.
3. Turn saucepan handles inward on the stovetop.
4. Ask Mom or Dad to show you how to operate appliances before you start.
5. Wear well-insulated oven mitts when handling hot plates and dishes.
6. Turn off burners and the oven and unplug small appliances when you're not using them.

Invite your parents to cook with you and help you handle sharp knives and hot pots and pans.

Be sure to keep your welcome in the kitchen by always cleaning up. Can kids cook? You bet they can! And with the *Kids Cook! 3-in-1 Cookbook Collection*, it's never been easier. Make it deliciously fun!

A note to parents: This book is intended for your 8- to 15-year-old children. Please supervise them when necessary. The handling of sharp knives, boiling liquids and hot pans needs to be monitored carefully with younger children.

Bag Lunches

Mix & Match
Bag Lunch Suggestions

BREADS	FRUIT	VEGETABLES
Bagels	Apple Raisin Bars*	Raisins
Bread Sticks	Apricot Logs*	Bean & Tomato Salad*

Buns:
   Dinner
   Hamburger
   Hot Dog
   Kaiser
   Submarine
	Banana Raisin Bars*
	
	Dried Fruit
	
	Fresh Fruit:
	   Apple
	   Banana
		Cottage Cheese Salad*
		Crunchy Potato Salad*
		Cucumber & Pea Salad*
		Cucumber Under Wraps*

English Muffins	Blueberries	Fresh Vegetables:

Loaves:
   Cheese
   Enriched White
   100% Whole Wheat
   Raisin
   Rye
   Seven-Grain
   60% Whole Wheat
	Cantaloupe
	   Grapefruit Sections
	   Grapes
	   Kiwifruit
	   Melon
	   Nectarine
	   Orange
	   Peach
		Asparagus
		   Broccoli
		   Carrot Sticks
		   Cauliflower
		   Celery Sticks
		   Cherry Tomatoes
		   Cucumber

Melba Toast	Pear
	   Plum
		Green Beans
		   Lettuce

Muffins:
   Apple Granola*
   Date & Nut*
	Raspberries
	   Strawberries
		Radishes
		   Tomato
		   Zucchini

Pepper Cheese Roll*	Frozen Bananas*	Rice Salad*
Pita Bread Pickly Pita Pockets*	Frozen Grapes* Frozen Oranges*	Salad Lunch* Tomato & Mozza Salad*
Soft Pretzel	Fruit Juice	Tortellini Salad*

Tortillas:
   Peanut Butter Wrap*
   "Wurst" Cheese &
      Lettuce Wrap*
	Fruit Salad*	Vegetable Juice
		
		Vegetable Roll*

* Recipe is included in this book. See Index for page number.

MILK & DAIRY	MEATS	EXTRAS

Cheese Slices:
  Cheddar
  Gouda
  Mozzarella

Cottage Cheese

Dips:
  Caesar*
  Garlic Mustard*
  Honey Mustard*
  Stick*

Macaroni & Cottage Cheese*

Milk:
  Homogenized
  2%
  1%
  Skim
  Chocolate

Yogurt (Plain or Fruit)

Cold Cooked Chicken/Turkey

Crispy Chicken Cracky*

Ham & Melon Kabobs*

Hamburger*

Hard-boiled Egg

Hero Sandwich*

Muffuletta*

Quick Turkey Loaf*

Roast Beef Rolls*

Sandwich Fillings:
  Baked Bean*
  Beef*
  Cheese*
  Cheese & Lettuce*
  Cheese & Tomato*
  Chicken*
  Egg
  Ham & Cheese*
  Ham & Cuke*
  Ham & Lettuce*
  Ham & Tomato*
  Peanut Butter*
  Peanut Butter & Pickle*
  Peanut Butter Banana*
  Salmon
  Tuna*
  Turkey

Super Sausage Sub*

Tuna Biscuits*

Tuna Buns*

Cookies:
  Butterscotch Pudding*
  Carrot*
  Corn Flakes Macaroons*
  Easy Raisin*
  Ginger Crinkles*
  Lemonade*
  Rolled Ginger*
  Snap Gingers*

Fruit Drink

Hot Dog*

Muffins:
  Lemon Blueberry*
  Orange Cranberry*

Pepper-Corn Crackers*

Snacks:
  Candied Popcorn*
  Citrus Crunchies*
  Corn Flakes Chews*
  Peanut Butter Popcorn
    Treats*
  Spiced Nuts*
  Summertime Snack Mix*
  Toasted Granola*
  Trail Mix

Squares:
  Butterscotch Bites*
  Chocolate Chip
    Granola Bars*
  Crispy Rice*
  Iced Crispy Rice*
  Puffed Wheat Candy*
  Puffed Wheat*
  Simple Chocolate Fudge*
  Sweet Ending Pizza*

* Recipe is included in this book. See Index for page number.

"Wurst" Cheese & Lettuce Wrap, page 68

Bag Lunches mix & match

Bag Lunches

A standard, healthy bag lunch should contain a grain product, some fruit or vegetables, a milk or dairy product and a meat or meat alternative. Add something extra for energy needs or for a special treat. To save time in the morning, prepare your lunch the night before and chill it in the refrigerator.

Check the Sandwiches section, pages 50 and 51, for a variety of sandwich and sandwich filling recipes. Combine these with the bread choices in the Bag Lunch Suggestions chart on pages 10 and 11 and you will never get bored. The snacks, cookies, candy and squares recipes in this book will make your lunch complete.

Consider how to keep meat and milk products cold. Placing a carton of frozen juice in the bottom of your lunch bag will keep your meat or fish sandwich safe to eat until lunchtime and makes a nice slushy drink. A small freezer pack works well, too, or try the following:

FROZEN BANANA: Peel a banana. Cut in half crosswise. Insert a flat wooden popsicle stick about halfway into each end. Place each half in a plastic container or resealable bag. Freeze. Include one in your lunch.

FROZEN GRAPES: Freeze a handful of seedless red or green grapes in a plastic container or resealable bag. Include them in your lunch. They will still be cold when it's lunchtime.

FROZEN ORANGES: Cut an orange into quarters. Put them in a plastic container or resealable bag. Freeze. Include them in your lunch.

Ginger Crinkles

GET READY ✔

dry measures, measuring spoons, liquid measures, large bowl, electric mixer, mixing spoon, small bowl, cookie sheet, oven mitts, wire rack, pancake lifter, waxed paper

1.	Hard margarine, softened	1 cup	250 mL
	Granulated sugar	1½ cups	375 mL
	Large egg	1	1
	Dark corn syrup	2 tbsp.	30 mL
	Molasses	½ cup	125 mL
2.	All-purpose flour	3 cups	750 mL
	Baking soda	2 tsp.	10 mL
	Ground cinnamon	2 tsp.	10 mL
	Ground ginger	1 tsp.	5 mL
	Ground cloves	¼ tsp.	1 mL
	Salt	½ tsp.	2 mL
3.	Granulated sugar, for coating	¼ cup	60 mL

Sure to be one of your favorites.

1. Place the oven rack in the centre position. Turn the oven on to 375°F (190°C). Measure the first 5 ingredients into the large bowl. Beat with the electric mixer on low speed until blended. Beat on medium speed until smooth.

2. Add the next 6 ingredients. Stir with the mixing spoon until moistened. Roll into 1½ inch (3.8 cm) balls.

3. Put the second amount of sugar into the small bowl. Roll the balls, 1 at a time, in the sugar until completely coated. Arrange the balls 2 inches (5 cm) apart on the ungreased cookie sheet. Bake in the oven for 12 to 14 minutes. Use the oven mitts to remove the cookie sheet to the wire rack. Let stand for 2 minutes. Use the pancake lifter to remove the cookies to the waxed paper on the counter. Cool completely. Makes about 3½ dozen (42) cookies.

Pictured at left and on page 13.

This is a very easy cookie to make because it uses a cake mix.

Easy Raisin Cookies

GET READY ✔

cookie sheet, liquid measures, measuring spoons, dry measures, large bowl, mixing spoon, oven mitts, wire rack, pancake lifter, waxed paper

1.			
Yellow cake mix (2 layer size)	1	1	
Large eggs, fork-beaten	2	2	
Cooking oil	⅓ cup	75 mL	
Water	2 tbsp.	30 mL	
Raisins	1 cup	250 mL	

1. Place the oven rack in the centre position. Turn the oven on to 350°F (175°C). Grease the cookie sheet. Combine all 5 ingredients with the mixing spoon in the bowl until moistened and smooth. Small lumps are fine. Drop by tablespoonfuls onto the cookie sheet. Bake in the oven for 18 minutes until golden brown. Use the oven mitts to remove the cookie sheet to the wire rack. Let stand for 2 minutes. Use the pancake lifter to remove the cookies to the waxed paper on the counter. Cool completely. Makes about 3½ dozen (42) cookies.

Careful or the adults will eat all of these.

Corn Flakes Macaroons

GET READY ✔

waxed paper, cookie sheet, large bowl, electric mixer, dry measures, measuring spoons, rubber spatula, oven mitts, wire rack, pancake lifter

1.	Egg whites (large), room temperature	3	3
2.	Granulated sugar	²/₃ cup	150 mL
	Vanilla flavouring	1 tsp.	5 mL
	Corn flakes cereal	2 cups	500 mL
	Fancy flake coconut	1 cup	250 mL

1. Place the oven rack in the centre position. Turn the oven on to 325°F (160°C). Lay the waxed paper on the ungreased cookie sheet. Beat the egg whites in the bowl with the electric mixer on high speed until foamy.

2. Gradually add the sugar while beating. Add the vanilla. Beat until shiny and stiff peaks form. Fold in the cereal and coconut using the spatula. Drop by tablespoonfuls onto the cookie sheet. Bake in the oven for 20 minutes until lightly browned and crisp. Use the oven mitts to remove the cookie sheet to the wire rack. Let stand for 2 minutes. Use the pancake lifter to remove the cookies to the waxed paper on the counter. Cool completely. Makes about 2¹/₂ dozen (30) cookies.

Butterscotch Pudding Cookies

GET READY ✔

measuring spoons, dry measures, medium bowl, mixing spoon, cookie sheet, table fork, oven mitts, wire rack, pancake lifter, waxed paper

1.
Hard margarine, melted	2 tbsp.	30 mL
Large egg, fork-beaten	1	1
Instant butterscotch pudding powder (4 serving size)	1	1
Biscuit mix	1 cup	250 mL
Milk	1 tbsp.	15 mL

1. Place the oven rack in the centre position. Turn the oven on to 350°F (175°C). Combine all 5 ingredients with the mixing spoon in the bowl. Shape the dough into balls, using 1 tbsp. (15 mL) dough for each. Place 3 inches (7 cm) apart on the ungreased cookie sheet. Make a crisscross pattern with the fork on top of each ball while lightly pressing down. Bake in the oven for 8 minutes. Use the oven mitts to remove the cookie sheet to the wire rack. Let stand for 2 minutes. Use the pancake lifter to remove the cookies to the waxed paper on the counter. Cool completely. Makes about 1½ dozen (18) cookies.

Variation: Add ½ cup (125 mL) chopped pecans or walnuts.

A very fast and easy way to make cookies.

Lemonade Cookies

GET READY ✔

cookie sheet, dry measures, medium bowl, mixing spoon, measuring spoons, small bowl, oven mitts, wire rack, pancake lifter, waxed paper, pastry brush

1. Hard margarine, softened   1 cup   250 mL
   Granulated sugar   1 cup   250 mL
   Large eggs   2   2
   Frozen concentrated lemonade   4 tbsp.   60 mL

2. All-purpose flour   3 cups   750 mL
   Baking soda   1 tsp.   5 mL
   Salt   ½ tsp.   2 mL

1. Place the oven rack in the centre position. Turn the oven on to 375°F (190°C). Grease the cookie sheet. Cream the margarine and sugar with the mixing spoon in the medium bowl. Beat in the eggs, 1 at a time. Add 2 tbsp. (30 mL) concentrated lemonade.

2. Stir the flour, baking soda and salt in the small bowl. Add to the egg mixture. Mix well. Drop by tablespoonfuls onto the cookie sheet. Bake in the oven for 10 to 12 minutes until light brown. Use the oven mitts to remove the cookie sheet to the wire rack. Let stand for 2 minutes. Use the pancake lifter to remove the cookies to the waxed paper on the counter. Use the pastry brush to brush the tops of the cookies with the remaining 2 tbsp. (30 mL) concentrated lemonade. Cool completely. Makes about 5 dozen (60) cookies.

Pictured on page 19.

Carrot Cookies

GET READY ✔

cookie sheet, dry measures, large bowl, mixing spoon, liquid measures, measuring spoons, oven mitts, wire rack, pancake lifter, waxed paper

1.	Hard margarine, softened	½ cup	125 mL
	Granulated sugar	1 cup	250 mL
	Large egg	1	1
	Cooked mashed carrot (or fresh, grated)	1 cup	250 mL
	Milk	⅓ cup	75 mL
	Vanilla flavouring	1 tsp.	5 mL
2.	All-purpose flour	2 cups	500 mL
	Rolled oats (not instant)	2 cups	500 mL
	Baking powder	2 tsp.	10 mL
	Salt	¼ tsp.	1 mL
	Ground cinnamon	1 tsp.	5 mL
	Raisins	1 cup	250 mL

1. Place the oven rack in the centre position. Turn the oven on to 375°F (190°C). Grease the cookie sheet. Cream the margarine and sugar well with the mixing spoon in the bowl. Beat in the egg. Add the carrot, milk and vanilla.

2. Add the remaining 6 ingredients. Mix well. Drop by tablespoonfuls onto the cookie sheet. Bake in the oven for 12 to 15 minutes until lightly browned. Use the oven mitts to remove the cookie sheet to the wire rack. Let stand for 2 minutes. Use the pancake lifter to remove the cookies to the waxed paper on the counter. Cool completely. Makes about 4 dozen (48) cookies.

The Carrot Cookies, shown at the top, use leftover or fresh carrots. The Lemonade Cookies, shown at the bottom, are made using frozen concentrated lemonade.

19

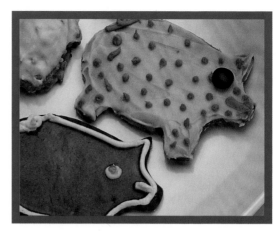

You will have fun making these Rolled Ginger Cookies. Use different cookie cutters to make an assortment of shapes. This recipe is great for making cookies for any special occasion.

Rolled Ginger Cookies

GET READY ✔

cookie sheet, dry measures, large bowl, mixing spoon, liquid measures, measuring spoons, cookie cutters, oven mitts, wire rack, pancake lifter, waxed paper

1.			
Hard margarine, softened	¼ cup	60 mL
Granulated sugar	½ cup	125 mL
Fancy (mild) molasses	½ cup	125 mL
Water	⅓ cup	75 mL

2.			
All-purpose flour	3¼ cups	800 mL
Baking soda	1 tsp.	5 mL
Ground ginger	1 tsp.	5 mL
Ground cinnamon	½ tsp.	2 mL
Ground cloves	¼ tsp.	1 mL
Salt	½ tsp.	2 mL

1. Place the oven rack in the centre position. Turn the oven on to 350°F (175°C). Grease the cookie sheet. Cream the margarine and sugar with the mixing spoon in the bowl. Add the molasses and water.

2. Mix in the remaining 6 ingredients. Roll out to ⅛ inch (3 mm) thickness on lightly floured surface. Cut out shapes with the cookie cutters. Place on the cookie sheet. Bake in the oven for 8 to 10 minutes. Use the oven mitts to remove the cookie sheet to the wire rack. Let stand for 2 minutes. Use the pancake lifter to remove the cookies to the waxed paper on the counter. Cool completely. Makes about 3 dozen (36) cookies.

Snap Gingers

GET READY ✔

dry measures, medium bowl, mixing spoon, liquid measures, rubber spatula, measuring spoons, cookie sheet, drinking glass, oven mitts, wire rack, pancake lifter, waxed paper

1.	Hard margarine, softened	½ cup	125 mL
	Granulated sugar	⅔ cup	150 mL
2.	Fancy (mild) molasses	¼ cup	60 mL
	Large egg, fork-beaten	1	1
3.	All-purpose flour	1½ cups	375 mL
	Baking soda	1½ tsp.	7 mL
	Ground ginger	1½ tsp.	7 mL
	Salt	¼ tsp.	1 mL
4.	Granulated sugar, for coating		

1. Place the oven rack in the centre position. Turn the oven on to 375°F (190°C). Cream the margarine and first amount of sugar well with the mixing spoon in the bowl.

2. Stir in the molasses and egg until well mixed, occasionally scraping down the sides of the bowl with the rubber spatula.

3. Stir in the next 4 ingredients until well blended.

4. Shape the dough into 1 inch (2.5 cm) balls. Roll each ball in the second amount of sugar until well coated. Place the balls 2 inches (5 cm) apart on the ungreased cookie sheet. Flatten each ball with the bottom of the glass to ¼ inch (6 mm) thickness. Bake in the oven for 7 minutes. Use the oven mitts to remove the cookie sheet to the wire rack. Let stand for 1 minute. Use the pancake lifter to remove the cookies to the waxed paper on the counter. Cool completely. Makes about 2 dozen (24) cookies.

A chewy cookie with ginger flavour through and through.

Stick Dip

GET READY ✔

measuring spoons, small bowl, mixing spoon

1. Sour cream | 3 tbsp. | 50 mL
   Beef bouillon powder | ½ tsp. | 2 mL
   Onion salt | ¼ tsp. | 1 mL

1. Combine all 3 ingredients with the mixing spoon in the bowl. Makes 3 tbsp. (50 mL) dip.

   Pictured on page 13.

Garlic Mustard Dip

GET READY ✔

dry measures, measuring spoons, small bowl, mixing spoon, plastic wrap

1. Salad dressing (or mayonnaise) | ⅓ cup | 75 mL
   Sour cream | ⅔ cup | 150 mL
   Prepared mustard | 1 tbsp. | 15 mL
   Garlic powder | ⅛ tsp. | 0.5 mL
   Salt, sprinkle
   Pepper, sprinkle

1. Combine all 6 ingredients with the mixing spoon in the bowl. Cover with plastic wrap. Chill for 30 minutes to blend the flavours. Makes 1¼ cups (300 mL) dip.

Garlic Mustard Dip is great with fresh veggies.

Honey Mustard Dunk

GET READY ✔

dry measures, measuring spoons, small bowl, mixing spoon

1.	Salad dressing (or mayonnaise)	½ cup	125 mL
	Liquid honey	2 tbsp.	30 mL
	Prepared mustard	2 tsp.	10 mL

1. Combine all 3 ingredients with the mixing spoon in the bowl until smooth. Makes ⅔ cup (150 mL) dip.

The next time you have fresh veggies for a snack, try Honey Mustard Dunk, shown at the top, or Caesar Dip, shown at the bottom.

Caesar Dip

GET READY ✔

dry measures, measuring spoons, small bowl, mixing spoon

1.	Salad dressing (or mayonnaise)	½ cup	125 mL
	Sour cream	½ cup	125 mL
	Lemon juice	1 tbsp.	15 mL
	Garlic clove, crushed (or ¼ tsp., 1 mL, powder)	1	1
	Salt	⅛ tsp.	0.5 mL
	Pepper	⅛ tsp.	0.5 mL
	Prepared mustard	1 tsp.	5 mL
	Grated Parmesan cheese	1 tbsp.	15 mL
	Parsley flakes	1 tsp.	5 mL

1. Combine all 9 ingredients with the mixing spoon in the bowl until smooth. Let stand for 15 minutes to blend the flavors. Makes ¾ cup (175 mL) dip.

Pepper-Corn Crackers

GET READY ✔

dry measures, measuring spoons, medium bowl, mixing spoon, pastry blender, cookie sheet, table fork, oven mitts, wire rack

1.	All-purpose flour	¾ cup	175 mL
	Corn flakes cereal	3 cups	750 mL
	Baking powder	¼ tsp.	1 mL
	Grated Cheddar (or Gouda or Edam or Monterey Jack) cheese	2 cups	500 mL
2.	Hard margarine	½ cup	125 mL
3.	Finely diced red pepper	½ cup	125 mL
4.	Paprika, sprinkle		

A soft and chewy cracker. A perfect addition to your lunch. These freeze well.

1. Place the oven rack in the centre position. Turn the oven on to 350°F (175°C). Combine the flour, cereal and baking powder with the mixing spoon in the bowl. Add the cheese. Stir well.

2. Cut in the margarine with the pastry blender until the mixture looks crumbly, with pieces no bigger than the size of a small pea. The mixture should almost want to stick together.

3. Work with your hands until a stiff dough forms. Work in the red pepper.

4. Shape the dough into 1 inch (2.5 cm) balls. Place the balls on the ungreased cookie sheet. Make a crisscross pattern with the fork on top of each ball while lightly pressing down. Sprinkle with the paprika. Bake in the oven for 15 minutes until golden brown. Use the oven mitts to remove the baking sheet to the wire rack. Cool completely. Makes 40 crackers.

Crispy Chicken Cracky

GET READY ✓

baking sheet, sharp knife, cutting board, medium bowl, dry measures, microwave-safe bowl, measuring spoons, mixing spoon, plastic freezer bag, oven mitts, wire rack

1.	Boneless, skinless chicken breast halves (about 1 lb., 454 g)	4	4
2.	Margarine	¼ cup	60 mL
	Worcestershire sauce (optional)	1 tsp.	5 mL
	Salt	½ tsp.	2 mL
	Pepper	¼ tsp.	1 mL
3.	Soda cracker crumbs (see Note)	⅔ cup	150 mL

1. Place the oven rack in the centre position. Turn the oven on to 400°F (205°C). Lightly grease the baking sheet. Cut each chicken breast with the knife into 6 chunks on the cutting board. Place in the medium bowl.

2. Microwave the margarine in the microwave-safe bowl on high (100%) for about 30 seconds until melted. Add the Worcestershire sauce, salt and pepper. Stir with the mixing spoon. Drizzle the margarine mixture over the chicken. Stir until well coated.

3. Put the cracker crumbs into the bag. Put 3 or 4 pieces of chicken at a time into the crumbs, shaking until well coated. Place the coated chicken on the baking sheet. Bake in the oven for 18 to 20 minutes until crisp and golden brown. Use the oven mitts to remove the baking sheet to the wire rack. Cool. Makes 24 chunks.

Note: To make crumbs, place the crackers in a plastic freezer bag. Roll with a rolling pin.

Eat hot or cold with Garlic Mustard Dip, page 22, or Honey Mustard Dunk, page 23.

Ham & Melon Kabobs

GET READY ✔

six 4 inch (10 cm) wooden bamboo skewers (or cocktail picks)

1.	Cantaloupe cubes (¾ inch, 2 cm, size)	12	12
	Ham cubes (¾ inch, 2 cm, size)	6	6

1. Push 1 cube of the cantaloupe, 1 cube of the ham, and another cube of cantaloupe on each skewer. Makes 6 kabobs.

Variation: 6 pieces of shaved ham, rolled or folded into 1 inch (2.5 cm) pieces, may be substituted for the ham cubes.

Pack in a covered container to take to school.

This is perfect for sandwich meat. Slices well when cold. Freeze individual slices for your lunch.

Quick Turkey Loaf

GET READY ✔
9 × 5 × 3 inch (22 × 12.5 × 7.5 cm) loaf pan, dry measures, measuring spoons, blender, large bowl, mixing spoon, oven mitts, wire rack

1.	Large egg	1	1
	Ketchup	⅓ cup	75 mL
	Seasoning salt	1½ tsp.	7 mL
	Pepper	⅛ tsp.	0.5 mL
	Small onion, cut into chunks	1	1
	Large carrot, cut into chunks	1	1
	Large celery rib, cut into chunks	1	1
2.	Lean ground turkey (or chicken)	1½ lbs.	680 g
	Large flake rolled oats (old-fashioned)	⅔ cup	150 mL

1. Place the oven rack in the centre position. Turn the oven on to 350°F (175°C). Grease the loaf pan. Combine the egg, ketchup, seasoning salt and pepper in the blender. Place the lid on the blender. Process until smooth. While the blender is processing, gradually add the onion, carrot and celery, a few pieces at a time, through the opening in the lid. Process until almost smooth. There will be some very small chunks of vegetable remaining.

2. Put the ground turkey into the bowl. Add the vegetable mixture. Stir well with the mixing spoon. Stir in the rolled oats. Let stand for 10 minutes. Pack into the loaf pan. Bake in the oven for 1¼ hours. Use the oven mitts to remove the pan to the wire rack. Let stand for 5 minutes. Cuts into 10 slices.

Macaroni & Cottage Cheese

GET READY ✔

liquid measures, measuring spoons, medium saucepan, dry measures, long-handled mixing spoon, colander, frying pan

1.
Water	4 cups	1 L
Salt	1 tsp.	5 mL
Elbow macaroni (or small shell pasta), uncooked	1½ cups	375 mL

2.
Margarine	2 tsp.	10 mL
Finely chopped onion	⅓ cup	75 mL
Imitation bacon bits (or 1 bacon slice, cooked crisp and crumbled)	1 tbsp.	15 mL
Creamed cottage cheese	1¼ cups	300 mL
Salt, sprinkle		
Pepper, sprinkle		

A new twist to an old favorite.

1. Bring the water and first amount of salt to a boil in the saucepan. Add the macaroni. Boil, uncovered, for 7 to 9 minutes, stirring occasionally, just until tender. Drain the pasta in the colander. Rinse with hot water. Drain. Return the pasta to the saucepan. Cover to keep warm.

2. Melt the margarine in the frying pan. Add the onion. Sauté using the mixing spoon until soft and golden brown. Add the bacon bits. Add the onion mixture to the pasta. Stir in the cottage cheese. Sprinkle with the second amount of salt and pepper. Cool. Reheat in the microwave at school. Makes 4 cups (1 L) mac and cheese.

Pickles add a delicious crunch. Eat now or cover and chill overnight for tomorrow's lunch.

Pickly Pita Pockets

GET READY ✔

dry measures, measuring spoons, small bowl, mixing spoon

1.	Diced ham (or beef roast or salami)	1 cup	250 mL
	Finely chopped dill pickle, blotted dry with paper towel	⅓ cup	75 mL
	Salad dressing (or mayonnaise)	2 tbsp.	30 mL
	Prepared mustard	1 tsp.	5 mL
2.	Pita breads (6 inch, 15 cm, size), cut in half	2	2

1. Combine the ham, pickle, salad dressing and mustard with the mixing spoon in the bowl.

2. Fill each pita half with ⅓ cup (75 mL) filling. Makes 4 pita halves.

Pictured on page 3 and above.

Cake mix makes a very easy start to these muffins.

Lemon Blueberry Muffins

GET READY ✓

18 muffin papers, 2 muffin pans (for 18 muffins), dry measures, large bowl, mixing spoon, rubber spatula, wooden toothpick, oven mitts, wire rack

1.	Lemon cake mix (2 layer size)	1	1
	Large eggs, fork-beaten	2	2
	Sour cream	1½ cups	375 mL
2.	Frozen blueberries	2 cups	500 mL

1. Place the oven rack in the centre position. Turn the oven on to 325°F (160°C). Place the muffin papers in the pans. Combine the cake mix, eggs and sour cream in the bowl. Stir with the mixing spoon until well blended. The batter will be stiff.

2. Lightly fold in the blueberries with the spatula. Divide the batter among the 18 muffin cups. Bake in the oven for 40 minutes until golden brown. The toothpick inserted in the centre of 2 or 3 muffins should come out clean. Use the oven mitts to remove the muffin pans to the wire rack. Let stand for 10 minutes. Remove the muffins to the rack to cool completely. Makes 18 muffins.

Date & Nut Muffins

GET READY ✔

muffin pan (for 12 muffins), dry measures, measuring spoons, large bowl, mixing spoon, liquid measures, blender, wooden toothpick, oven mitts, wire rack

1.			
All-purpose flour	1½ cups	375 mL
Whole-wheat flour	½ cup	125 mL
Baking powder	1 tbsp.	15 mL
Brown sugar, packed	¼ cup	60 mL
Chopped walnuts	½ cup	125 mL
2.		
Milk	1 cup	250 mL
Large egg	1	1
Cooking oil	¼ cup	60 mL
Maple flavouring	½ tsp.	2 mL
Chopped dates	½ cup	125 mL

1. Place the oven rack in the centre position. Turn the oven on to 375°F (190°C). Grease the muffin pan. Combine the first 5 ingredients with the mixing spoon in the bowl. Make a well in the centre.

2. Measure the remaining 5 ingredients into the blender. Place the lid on the blender. Process for 5 to 10 seconds. Pour the wet ingredients into the well in the flour mixture. Stir just to moisten. Divide the batter among the 12 muffin cups. Bake in the oven for 20 minutes until golden brown. The toothpick inserted in the centre of 2 or 3 muffins should come out clean. Use the oven mitts to remove the muffin pan to the wire rack. Let stand for 10 minutes. Remove the muffins to the rack to cool completely. Makes 12 muffins.

A great snack for any time of the day.

Orange Cranberry Muffins

GET READY ✓

muffin pan (for 12 muffins), sharp knife, cutting board, blender, liquid measures, dry measures, measuring spoons, large bowl, mixing spoon, wooden toothpick, oven mitts, wire rack

1.			
	Medium navel orange, washed	1	1
	Prepared orange juice	½ cup	125 mL
	Large egg	1	1
	Hard margarine	½ cup	125 mL
	Dried cranberries	½ cup	125 mL
2.	All-purpose flour	1¾ cups	425 mL
	Baking powder	1 tsp.	5 mL
	Baking soda	1 tsp.	5 mL
	Granulated sugar	⅔ cup	150 mL
	Salt	½ tsp.	2 mL

Using the entire orange gives these muffins lots of vitamins and minerals.

1. Place the oven rack in the centre position. Turn the oven on to 400°F (205°C). Grease the muffin pan. Cut the orange with the knife into 8 pieces on the cutting board. Put into the blender. Add the orange juice. Place the lid on the blender. Process for 1½ minutes until the orange peel is finely chopped. Add the egg and margarine. Process until blended. Add the dried cranberries. Process for 2 seconds.

2. Combine the remaining 5 ingredients with the mixing spoon in the large bowl. Make a well in the centre. Pour the wet ingredients into the well. Stir just to moisten. Divide the batter among the 12 muffin cups. Bake in the oven for 15 minutes until golden brown. The toothpick inserted in the centre of 2 or 3 muffins should come out clean. Use the oven mitts to remove the muffin pan to the wire rack. Let stand for 10 minutes. Remove the muffins to the rack to cool completely. Makes 12 muffins.

Moist and delicious.

Apple Granola Muffins

GET READY ✔

muffin pan (for 12 muffins), dry measures, measuring spoons, medium bowl, mixing spoon, pastry blender, liquid measures, wooden toothpick, oven mitts, wire rack

1.			
	All-purpose flour	2 cups	500 mL
	Baking powder	4 tsp.	20 mL
	Salt	1 tsp.	5 mL
	Brown sugar, packed	3 tbsp.	50 mL
	Ground cinnamon	½ tsp.	2 mL
2.	Hard margarine	⅓ cup	75 mL
	Medium apple, cored and chopped	1	1
	Milk	1 cup	250 mL
	Vanilla flavouring	1 tsp.	5 mL
3.	Granola cereal	¼ cup	60 mL

1. Place the oven rack in the centre position. Turn the oven on to 400°F (205°C). Grease the muffin pan. Combine the first 5 ingredients with the mixing spoon in the bowl.

2. Cut the margarine in with the pastry blender until the mixture looks crumbly. Add the apple, milk and vanilla. Stir just to moisten. Divide the batter among the 12 muffin cups.

3. Sprinkle each with 1 tsp. (5 mL) cereal. Bake in the oven for 20 minutes until golden brown. The toothpick inserted in the centre of 2 or 3 muffins should come out clean. Use the oven mitts to remove the muffin pan to the wire rack. Let stand for 10 minutes. Remove the muffins to the rack to cool completely. Makes 12 muffins.

So colourful, juicy and tasty. Choose from a variety of fresh fruits. Do not freeze.

Fruit Salad

GET READY ✔

covered container, mixing spoon

1.			
Watermelon chunks	6	6	
Kiwifruit slices, cut in half	3	3	
Cantaloupe chunks	4	4	
Orange segments, cut in half	3	3	
Seedless red or green grapes (or both)	6	6	
Apple (or pear) slices (or both),	3	3	
dipped into fruit (or lemon) juice			
to keep from browning			

1. Combine all 6 ingredients in the container. Stir with the mixing spoon. Place the lid on the container. Makes about 2 cups (500 mL) salad.

Salad Lunch

GET READY ✔

medium covered container, small covered container

1.			
Chopped iceberg lettuce	½ cup	125 mL
Tomato wedges	2	2
Cucumber slices	3	3
Celery stick	1	1
1 inch (2.5 cm) cubes of Cheddar cheese	2	2
Thin carrot sticks	3	3
Large hard-boiled egg	½	½

2. Stick Dip, page 22

1. Put the first 7 ingredients into the medium container. Place the lid on the container.
2. Put the dip into the small container. Place the lid on the container. Serves 1.

Cottage Cheese Salad

GET READY ✔

dry measures, measuring spoons, small bowl, mixing spoon

1.			
Creamed cottage cheese	1 cup	250 mL
Diced cucumber, with peel	¼ cup	60 mL
Grated carrot	2 tbsp.	30 mL
Diced red pepper	2 tbsp.	30 mL
Garlic salt	⅛ tsp.	0.5 mL
Pepper, sprinkle		
Celery seed, sprinkle		

1. Combine all 7 ingredients with the mixing spoon in the bowl. Let stand for 10 minutes to blend the flavours. Chill for up to 24 hours. Makes 1½ cups (375 mL) salad.

Very colourful. A great blend of flavours.

A colourful and tasty salad.

Tortellini Salad

GET READY ✔
liquid measures, measuring spoons, small saucepan, dry measures, colander, medium bowl, mixing spoon, plastic wrap

1.			
	Water	6 cups	1.5 L
	Salt	1 tsp.	5 mL
	Fresh (or dried) cheese-filled tortellini	1 cup	250 mL
2.	Diced cucumber, with peel	½ cup	125 mL
	Small tomato, diced	1	1
	Thinly sliced green onion	¼ cup	60 mL
	Thinly slivered green or red pepper	½ cup	125 mL
	Salt	½ tsp.	2 mL
	Pepper	⅛ tsp.	0.5 mL

1. Bring the water and salt to a boil in the saucepan. Add the tortellini. Heat for about 10 minutes until tender but still firm. Drain in the colander. Rinse with cold water until cool. Drain well.

2. Combine the pasta and the remaining 6 ingredients with the mixing spoon in the bowl. Cover with plastic wrap. Chill for 30 minutes to blend the flavours. Makes 3½ cups (875 mL) salad.

Bean & Tomato Salad

GET READY ✔

dry measures, medium bowl, mixing spoon, measuring spoons, small bowl, plastic wrap

1.			
Can of garbanzo beans (chickpeas), drained and rinsed	19 oz.	540 mL	
Thinly sliced celery	½ cup	125 mL	
Green onion, thinly sliced	1	1	
Diced red pepper	½ cup	125 mL	
Can of stewed tomatoes, drained and chopped	14 oz.	398 mL	

2.	DRESSING		
Olive (or cooking) oil	2 tbsp.	30 mL	
White vinegar	2 tbsp.	30 mL	
Dried sweet basil	½ tsp.	2 mL	
Dry mustard	¼ tsp.	1 mL	
Garlic powder	⅛ tsp.	0.5 mL	
Parsley flakes	2 tsp.	10 mL	

1. Combine the first 5 ingredients with the mixing spoon in the medium bowl.

2. **Dressing:** Combine the remaining 6 ingredients in the small bowl. Pour over the vegetable mixture. Mix well. Cover with plastic wrap. Chill for several hours or overnight, stirring several times. Chill for up to 3 days. Makes 4 cups (1 L) salad.

A delicious, crunchy salad. Perfect to take to school for lunch.

Crunchy Potato Salad

GET READY ✔

sharp knife, cutting board, liquid measures, measuring spoons, small saucepan, colander, medium bowl, mixing spoon, plastic wrap

1.	Large potato	1	1
	Water	1 cup	250 mL
	Salt	¼ tsp.	1 mL
2.	Diced red pepper	2 tbsp.	30 mL
	Grated carrot	1 tbsp.	15 mL
	Finely diced celery	1 tbsp.	15 mL
	Sliced green onion	1 tbsp.	15 mL
	Grated Cheddar cheese	2 tbsp.	30 mL
	Italian dressing	2 tbsp.	30 mL
	Salt, sprinkle		
	Pepper, sprinkle		

1. Cut the potato crosswise with the knife into 3 pieces on the cutting board. Put the potato pieces, water and salt into the saucepan. Bring to a boil on high. Reduce the heat to low. Cover. Simmer for about 13 minutes until the potato is tender when poked with the knife. Do not overcook or the potato will be mushy. Drain in the colander. Cool slightly. Dice into small cubes on the cutting board.

2. Combine the potato and the remaining 8 ingredients with the mixing spoon in the bowl. Cover with plastic wrap. Chill until cold. Makes 1½ cups (375 mL) salad.

Very colourful. Watch the cooking time of the potato. It will differ according to the size of your potato.

Make this salad the night before to take to school the next day. A crunchy, refreshing salad.

Cucumber & Pea Salad

GET READY ✔

dry measures, measuring spoons, small bowl, mixing spoon, small cup

1.			
Diced cucumber, with peel	1 cup	250 mL
Frozen baby peas, thawed	½ cup	125 mL
Sliced green onion	2 tbsp.	30 mL
Garlic salt, sprinkle		
Pepper, sprinkle		
Cubed Cheddar (or Swiss) cheese (½ inch, 12 mm, size)	½ cup	125 mL

2.	DRESSING		
Salad dressing (or mayonnaise)	2 tbsp.	30 mL
Granulated sugar	2 tsp.	10 mL
Lemon juice	1 tsp.	5 mL

1. Combine the first 6 ingredients with the mixing spoon in the bowl.

2. **Dressing:** Mix the salad dressing, sugar and lemon juice in the cup. Add to the vegetable mixture. Mix well. Makes 2 cups (500 mL) salad.

Rice Salad

1.			
Cooked rice (your favorite)	¾ cup	175 mL
Cooked ham, chopped	2 oz.	57 g
Sliced green onion	2 tbsp.	30 mL
Cooked vegetables (such as peas, broccoli florets or green beans)	½ cup	125 mL
Grated carrot	¼ cup	60 mL
Olive (or cooking) oil	1 tsp.	5 mL
White (or red wine or apple cider) vinegar	2 tsp.	10 mL
Salt, sprinkle		

1. Combine all 8 ingredients with the mixing spoon in the bowl. Makes 1½ cups (375 mL) salad.

Variation: Add 2 tbsp. (30 mL) sunflower seeds or pumpkin seeds, or add ¼ cup (60 mL) raisins.

This salad can also be stuffed into a pita bread for a salad sandwich.

Tomato & Mozza Salad

GET READY ✔

sharp knife, cutting board, paper towel, small bowl, measuring spoons, mixing spoon, dry measures

1.	**Medium tomatoes**	2	2
2.	**Olive (or cooking) oil**	2 tsp.	10 mL
	Garlic salt	¼ tsp.	1 mL
	Pepper, sprinkle		
	Dried sweet basil	¼ tsp.	1 mL
	Sliced green onion	1 tbsp.	15 mL
	Ripe olives, sliced (optional)	4	4
3.	**Grated mozzarella cheese**	½ cup	125 mL

1. Cut the tomatoes in half with the knife on the cutting board. Gently squeeze the tomato halves over the paper towel to remove the seeds. Discard the seeds and juice. Dice the tomato into bite-size pieces. Place in the bowl.

2. Add the next 6 ingredients. Stir with the mixing spoon.

3. Stir in the cheese. Makes 1½ cups (375 mL) salad.

Variation: Spoon salad onto baguette slices. Place the slices on a baking sheet. Broil on the top rack in the oven until the cheese is melted.

This salad tastes even better when left to stand awhile. Great to take for lunch.

Pronounced muhf-ful-LEHT-tuh. Make this New Orleans sandwich the night before to take for lunch the next day.

Muffuletta

GET READY ✔
measuring spoons, small cup, pastry brush, dry measures

1.

Italian-style crusty bun, cut in half horizontally	1	1
Italian dressing	1½ tbsp.	25 mL
Tomato slices	4	4
Mozzarella cheese slices	2	2
Lean ham (or beef) slices (about 2 oz., 57 g)	2	2
Alfalfa sprouts (or shredded lettuce)	⅓ cup	75 mL

1. Pull out bits of bread from the soft centre of both bun halves, making a shallow hollow. Put the dressing into the cup. Use the pastry brush to spread about ½ tbsp. (7 mL) dressing on each bun half. Layer 2 slices of tomato, 1 slice of cheese and 1 slice of ham on the bottom half of the bun. Brush the remaining dressing on the ham. Top with the sprouts, remaining cheese slice, remaining tomato slices and remaining ham slice. Cover with the top half of the bun. Makes 1 sandwich.

Tuna Biscuits

GET READY ✔

muffin pan (for 8 large or 16 mini muffins), dry measures, measuring spoons, medium bowl, whisk, mixing spoon, oven mitts, wire rack

1.	Large eggs, fork-beaten	2	2
	Salad dressing (or mayonnaise)	¼ cup	60 mL
	Margarine, melted	2 tbsp.	30 mL
	Lemon juice	½ tbsp.	7 mL
	Hot pepper sauce	⅛ tsp.	0.5 mL
2.	Cheese-flavoured crackers, coarsely crushed	22	22
	Can of white tuna, packed in water, drained and broken into chunks	6½ oz.	184 g
	Green onion, sliced	1	1
	Finely diced green pepper (optional)	2 tbsp.	30 mL

1. Place the oven rack in the centre position. Turn the oven on to 375°F (190°C). Grease 8 large cups, or 16 mini cups, in the muffin pan. Combine the egg, salad dressing, margarine, lemon juice and hot pepper sauce in the bowl. Beat with the whisk until well blended.

2. Stir the cracker crumbs into the egg mixture with the mixing spoon. Add the tuna, green onion and green pepper. Stir well. Fill the muffin cups ¾ full with the batter. Bake in the oven for 20 minutes for the large cups or for 15 minutes for the mini cups. Use the oven mitts to remove the pan to the wire rack. Makes 8 large biscuits or 16 mini biscuits.

Very tasty. Great to take for lunch instead of a sandwich.

Yummy to eat for lunch any day of the week.

Ham & Cuke Sandwich

GET READY ✔

measuring spoons, small bowl, mixing spoon, table knife, bread knife, cutting board

1.			
Salad dressing (or mayonnaise)	2 tsp.	10 mL
French (or Russian) dressing	2 tsp.	10 mL
Whole-wheat (or white) bread slices	2	2

2.			
Shaved ham slices (about 2 oz., 57 g)	2	2
Cucumber slices, with peel	3-4	3-4

1. Combine the salad dressing and French dressing with the mixing spoon in the bowl. Spread the mixture on both slices of bread with the table knife.

2. Place the ham slices on 1 slice of bread. Top with the cucumber slices. Cover with the second slice of bread. Cut in half with the bread knife on the cutting board. Makes 1 sandwich.

Tuna Buns

GET READY ✔

measuring spoons, dry measures, medium bowl, mixing spoon, frying pan, pancake lifter, table knife

1. | Can of tuna in water, with liquid, flaked | 6½ oz. | 184 g |
   |---|---|---|
   | Large egg, fork-beaten | 1 | 1 |
   | Minced onion flakes | 1 tsp. | 5 mL |
   | Small carrot, grated | 1 | 1 |
   | Fine dry bread crumbs | ½ cup | 125 mL |
   | Parsley flakes | 1 tsp. | 5 mL |
   | Lemon juice | 1 tsp. | 5 mL |
   | Salt, sprinkle | | |
   | Pepper, sprinkle | | |

2. | Cooking oil | 1 tsp. | 5 mL |
   |---|---|---|

3. | Salad dressing (or mayonnaise) | 2 tbsp. | 30 mL |
   |---|---|---|
   | Kaiser rolls, cut in half horizontally | 4 | 4 |
   | Lettuce leaves | 4 | 4 |

1. Combine the first 9 ingredients with the mixing spoon in the bowl. Form into 4 patties.

2. Heat the cooking oil in the frying pan on medium. Put the patties into the frying pan. Cook the patties for about 2 minutes until golden brown. Turn the patties over with the pancake lifter. Cook for 2 minutes until golden brown and crispy.

3. Spread the salad dressing with the knife on the bottom half of each roll. Place 1 patty on top of the salad dressing. Top with the lettuce. Cover with the top halves of the rolls. Makes 4 buns.

Great warm or cold.

Pepper Cheese Roll

GET READY ✔

bread knife, cutting board, measuring spoons, pastry brush, dry measures

1.	Whole-wheat roll, oblong (or oval) shaped (about 5 inches, 12.5 cm, long)	1	1
	Italian dressing	1 tbsp.	15 mL
2.	Red, orange or yellow pepper, cut into thin strips	½	½
	Pepper, sprinkle		
	Dried sweet basil, just a pinch		
	White cheese (such as mozzarella, Swiss or Monterey Jack), thinly sliced	2 oz.	57 g
	Alfalfa (or mixed) sprouts (optional)	¼ cup	60 mL

1.   Cut the roll in half horizontally with the bread knife on the cutting board. Pull out bits of bread from the soft centre of both roll halves, making a shallow hollow. Use the pastry brush to spread about ½ tbsp. (7 mL) dressing on each roll half.

2.   Lay the pepper strips lengthwise on the bottom half. Sprinkle with the pepper and basil. Lay the cheese slices on the pepper strips. Spread the sprouts on the cheese. Cover with the top half of the roll. Makes 1 sandwich.

This can be made ahead, wrapped with plastic wrap and chilled for up to two days.

These will freeze well. Simply thaw before heating, or pop in your lunch bag in the morning and by noon the sub is well thawed. A great lunch!

Super Sausage Sub

GET READY ✓

non-stick frying pan, long-handled mixing spoon, colander, measuring spoons, liquid measures, dry measures

1.	Ground sausage meat	1 lb.	454 g
	Medium green pepper, cut into slivers	1	1
	Medium onion, sliced	1	1
	Pepper	⅛ tsp.	0.5 mL
	Paprika	½ tsp.	2 mL
	Cayenne pepper, sprinkle		
	Meatless spaghetti sauce	1 cup	250 mL
2.	Submarine buns (10 inches, 25 cm, long), cut in half horizontally	4	4
	Grated Cheddar (or mozzarella) cheese	1 cup	250 mL

1. Scramble-fry the sausage in the frying pan on medium for 10 minutes using the mixing spoon, breaking up any large lumps. Drain in the colander. Add the green pepper, onion, pepper, paprika and cayenne pepper. Scramble-fry for 10 minutes until the vegetables are tender-crisp and the sausage is no longer pink. Stir in the spaghetti sauce. Remove from the heat. Makes 3 cups (750 mL) sauce.

2. Pull out bits of bread from the soft centre of both bun halves, making a shallow hollow. Divide the sausage mixture among the 4 bottom halves of the buns. Top each with ¼ cup (60 mL) cheese. Cover with the top halves of the buns. Makes 4 sandwiches.

    Pictured on page 9 and above.

Variation: These can be heated in the microwave oven on medium (50%) for 1 minute or wrapped with foil and heated in a 300°F (150°C) oven for 15 minutes.

Hero Sandwich

GET READY ✔
bread knife, cutting board, measuring spoons, table knife

1.	Submarine bun (12 inches, 30 cm, long)	1	1
	Salad dressing (or mayonnaise)	1 tbsp.	15 mL
	Prepared mustard	2 tsp.	10 mL
2.	Thin slices of salami (about 1½ oz., 42 g)	6	6
	Thinly shaved deli ham (or chicken or turkey)	1½ oz.	42 g
	Tomato slices	5	5
	Mozzarella (or Monterey Jack) cheese, thinly sliced	2 oz.	57 g
	Shredded lettuce (or mixed sprouts)	½ cup	125 mL
	Salt, sprinkle		
	Pepper, sprinkle		

1. Cut the submarine bun in half horizontally on the cutting board with the bread knife. Pull out bits of bread from the soft centre of both bun halves, making a shallow hollow. Spread the salad dressing on each half with the table knife. Spread the mustard on the salad dressing.

2. Layer the next 5 ingredients on top of the mustard on bottom bun half in the order given. Sprinkle with the salt and pepper. Cover with the top half of the bun. Cut in half on the cutting board with the bread knife. Makes 1 sandwich.

You will be a hero if you can finish this! You will be an even bigger hero if you share!

Peanut Butter & Pickle Sandwich

GET READY ✔

measuring spoons, table knife, paper towel, bread knife, cutting board

1.	**Peanut butter**	**2 tbsp.**	**30 mL**
	White (or whole-wheat) bread slices	**2**	**2**
2.	**Dill pickle(s), cut in half lengthwise**	**1-2**	**1-2**

1. Spread the peanut butter with the table knife on 1 side of each bread slice.

2. Lay the pickle halves on the paper towel for 1 to 2 minutes to soak up the juice. Lay pickle halves on top of the peanut butter. Cover with the second slice of bread, peanut butter side down. Cut in half with the bread knife on the cutting board. Makes 1 sandwich.

Variation: Spread peanut butter on a flour tortilla. Lay a small whole dill pickle on top of the tortilla at 1 end. Roll the tortilla around the pickle.

Who would have thought! Sounds interesting—and very tasty!

Sandwiches

Baked Bean Sandwich: Spread drained beans (or drained and mashed) on 1 slice of buttered bread. Add some chopped cooked sausage, ground meat or wieners. Cover with the second slice of buttered bread.

Beef Sandwich: Spread mustard, ketchup or salad dressing (or mayonnaise) on 1 slice of buttered bread. Add slices of cold roast beef. Top with lettuce or alfalfa sprouts. The lettuce will stay crisper if on the side not touching the salad dressing. Cover with the second slice of buttered bread. See ❻ page 51.

Cheese & Lettuce Sandwich: Spread salad dressing (or mayonnaise) or sandwich spread on 1 slice of buttered bread. Lay a cheese slice on the salad dressing. Top with lettuce. The lettuce will stay crisper if on the side not touching the salad dressing. Cover with the second slice of buttered bread. See ❸ page 51.

Cheese & Tomato Sandwich: Spread salad dressing (or mayonnaise) or sandwich spread on 1 slice of buttered bread. Lay a cheese slice on top. Cover the cheese with tomato slices. Sprinkle with salt and pepper. Cover with the second slice of buttered bread. See ❺ page 51.

Cheese Sandwich: Lay a slice of Swiss or Cheddar cheese on 1 slice of buttered bread. Or spread with processed cheese spread. Cover with the second slice of buttered bread. See ❷ page 51.

Chicken Sandwich or Roll: Butter 2 slices of bread or the inside surfaces of a roll. Using leftover cooked chicken, slice enough to cover 1 bread slice. Either a bit of cranberry sauce or some leftover stuffing is a tasty addition. Cover with the second slice of buttered bread.

Ham & Cheese Sandwich: Spread mustard, salad dressing (or mayonnaise) or sandwich spread on 1 slice of buttered bread. Add a slice of ham and a slice of cheese. Cover with the second slice of buttered bread. See ❹ page 51. Also pictured on page 13.

Ham & Lettuce Sandwich: Spread mustard or salad dressing (or mayonnaise) on 1 slice of buttered bread. Put a slice of ham on top. Add some lettuce. The lettuce will stay crisper if on the side not touching the salad dressing. Cover with the second slice of buttered bread.

Ham & Tomato Sandwich: Spread mustard, salad dressing (or mayonnaise) or sandwich spread on 1 slice of buttered bread. Add a slice of ham and a slice of tomato. Cover with the second slice of buttered bread.

Hamburger: Lay a cooked meat patty on the bottom half of a buttered hamburger bun. Spread ketchup, mustard and relish on the top half of the bun. You can also add onions (raw or cooked), pickles, cheese slice or tomatoes.

Hot Dog: Lay a hot wiener on the bottom half of a buttered hot dog bun. Spread ketchup, relish and mustard on the top half. You can also add onions (raw or cooked), cheese (slice or grated) and a cooked strip of bacon. A delicious hot dog has a narrow slice of cheese and a slice of cooked bacon alongside of the wiener.

PBBS: Do try a Peanut Butter Banana Sandwich. Spread peanut butter on 1 slice of buttered bread. Place a layer of banana slices on top. Cover with the second slice of buttered bread. See ❶ above.

Peanut Butter Sandwich: Spread peanut butter on 1 slice of buttered bread. Cover with the second slice of buttered bread.

Submarine: Split and butter a submarine bun. Layer the bottom half with cheese slices, cold meat slices, tomato slices and lettuce. Spread salad dressing (or mayonnaise) and mustard on the top half of the bun. Cover with the top half of the bun.

Spiced Nuts

GET READY ✔

measuring spoons, 10 inch (25 cm) glass pie plate (or small microwave-safe casserole dish), mixing spoon, dry measures, oven mitts, hot pad, paper towel, large plate

1.	Margarine	2 tbsp.	30 mL
2.	Soy sauce	1 tsp.	5 mL
	Lemon juice	1 tsp.	5 mL
	Ground ginger	¼ tsp.	1 mL
	Garlic powder	⅛ tsp.	0.5 mL
	Onion powder	⅛ tsp.	0.5 mL
	Salt	¼ tsp.	1 mL
3.	Walnut (or pecan) halves	¾ cup	175 mL
	Whole blanched almonds	¾ cup	175 mL

1. Measure the margarine into the pie plate. Microwave on high (100%) for 20 to 30 seconds until melted.

2. Add the next 6 ingredients. Stir well with the mixing spoon.

3. Add the walnuts and almonds. Stir. Microwave on high (100%) for 2 minutes. Stir. Repeat in 2 minute intervals until the nuts are toasted. This will take about 10 minutes. Use the oven mitts to remove the pie plate to the hot pad. Lay the paper towel on the large plate. Use the oven mitts to turn out the nuts onto the paper towel to cool. Makes 1⅔ cups (400 mL).

Cool completely. Store any extra mixture in a covered container.

A sweet mix. You'll be popular if you share this with your friends.

Summertime Snack Mix

GET READY ✓
dry measures, large microwave-safe bowl, mixing spoon, measuring spoons, liquid measures, small bowl, oven mitts, hot pad

1.	Honey graham cereal squares	2 cups	500 mL
	"O"-shaped toasted oat cereal	2 cups	500 mL
	Dried banana chips	1 cup	250 mL
2.	Hard margarine, melted	3 tbsp.	50 mL
	Liquid honey	¼ cup	60 mL
	Ground cinnamon	½ tsp.	2 mL
	Lemon juice	2 tsp.	10 mL
3.	Chopped dried pineapple	1 cup	250 mL
	Light raisins	1 cup	250 mL
	Long thread coconut	1 cup	250 mL
	Popped corn (pop about 2 tbsp., 30 mL, kernels)	4 cups	1 L

1. Combine the first 3 ingredients with the mixing spoon in the large bowl.

2. Combine the melted margarine, honey, cinnamon and lemon juice in the small bowl. Stir. Pour the honey mixture slowly over the cereal mixture. Stir until well coated. Microwave, uncovered, on high (100%) for 2 minutes. Stir well. Microwave on high (100%) for 2 to 3 minutes, stirring at the end of each minute and watching so it does not burn. It should look toasted when done. Use the oven mitts to remove the bowl to the hot pad.

3. Add the pineapple, raisins, coconut and popcorn. Toss well. Let cool for about 1 hour. Makes 10 cups (2.5 L) snack mix.

    Pictured on page 2 and above.

Toasted Granola

GET READY ✔

dry measures, large bowl, long-handled mixing spoon, liquid measures, measuring spoons, 9 × 13 inch (22 × 33 cm) oblong baking pan, oven mitts, wire rack

1.			
	Large flake rolled oats (old-fashioned)	2 cups	500 mL
	Medium coconut	½ cup	125 mL
	Shelled roasted sunflower seeds	¼ cup	60 mL
	Finely chopped dried apricots	½ cup	125 mL
	Light raisins	½ cup	125 mL
	Bran flakes cereal, crushed	½ cup	125 mL
	Brown sugar, packed	⅓ cup	75 mL
2.	Cooking oil	¼ cup	60 mL
	Water	2 tbsp.	30 mL
	Vanilla (or almond) flavouring	1 tsp.	5 mL

Add any chopped dried fruits in place of the apricots and raisins.

1. Place the oven rack in the centre position. Turn the oven on to 300°F (150°C). Combine the first 7 ingredients with the mixing spoon in the bowl.

2. Combine the cooking oil, water and vanilla in a liquid measure. Stir. Pour the cooking oil mixture over the granola mixture. Stir well. Spread the granola mixture in the ungreased pan. Bake in the oven for 25 minutes, stirring frequently. Use the oven mitts to remove the pan to the wire rack. Cool. Makes 5 cups (1.25 L) snack mix.

Candied Popcorn

GET READY ✓

dry measures, measuring spoons, very large bowl, 2 long-handled mixing spoons, large microwave-safe bowl, waxed paper

1.	Popped corn (pop about ⅓ cup, 75 mL, kernels)	10 cups	2.5 L
	Corn flakes cereal	2 cups	500 mL
	Hard margarine, melted	2 tbsp.	30 mL
2.	Raspberry drink mix	¼ cup	60 mL
3.	Hard margarine	2 tbsp.	30 mL
	Large marshmallows	36	36
	Vanilla flavouring	1 tsp.	5 mL

1. Combine the popped corn, cereal and first amount of margarine with 1 of the mixing spoons in the very large bowl. Mix well.

2. Sprinkle the drink mix over the popcorn mixture. Stir until well coated.

3. Put the second amount of margarine and marshmallows into the microwave-safe bowl. Microwave on high (100%) for 1½ to 2 minutes. Stir until the marshmallows are melted. Add the vanilla. Stir. Grease both of the mixing spoons. Pour the hot marshmallow mixture over the popcorn mixture. Toss quickly with the greased spoons until lightly coated. Lay the waxed paper on the counter or working surface. Turn the popcorn mixture out onto the waxed paper. Separate into serving-size pieces. Let cool on the waxed paper for 30 minutes. Makes 13 cups (3.25 L) popcorn mix.

A sticky situation—but worth it!

Just a hint of peanut butter and sweetness.

Left: Peanut Butter Popcorn Treats
Right: Choco-Peanut Butter Popcorn Balls

Peanut Butter Popcorn Treats

GET READY ✔

dry measures, small saucepan, liquid measures, mixing spoon, hot pad, measuring spoons, large bowl, baking sheet, oven mitts, wire rack

1.	Margarine	¼ cup	60 mL
2.	Brown sugar, packed	½ cup	125 mL
	Corn syrup	⅔ cup	150 mL
3.	Smooth peanut butter	½ cup	125 mL
	Vanilla flavouring	1 tsp.	5 mL
4.	Popped corn (pop about ¼ cup, 60 mL, kernels)	8 cups	2 L

1. Place the oven rack in the centre position. Turn the oven on to 350°F (175°C). Melt the margarine in the saucepan on medium.

2. Add the brown sugar and corn syrup. Heat, stirring constantly with the mixing spoon, until the brown sugar is dissolved.

3. Stir in the peanut butter. Bring the mixture to a boil. Remove the saucepan to the hot pad. Stir in the vanilla flavouring.

4. Put the popcorn into the bowl. Pour the margarine mixture over the popcorn. Toss until well coated. Spread evenly on the ungreased baking sheet. Bake in the oven for 7 minutes. Use the oven mitts to remove the baking sheet to the wire rack. Cool. Break up the cooled popcorn into bite-size chunks. Makes 8 cups (2 L) popcorn mix.

CHOCO-PEANUT BUTTER POPCORN BALLS: Add 2 tbsp. (30 mL) cocoa powder along with the peanut butter to the dissolved brown sugar mixture in the saucepan. Bring to a boil. Remove the saucepan to the hot pad. Add the vanilla flavouring. Pour over the popcorn. Toss until well coated. Cool the popcorn mixture long enough so that you can handle it. Grease your hands. Shape the popcorn mixture into tennis-size balls. Place on the waxed paper to set. Makes about 14 balls.

Apricot Logs

GET READY ✔

dry measures, measuring spoons, medium microwave-safe casserole dish, blender, medium bowl, mixing spoon, waxed paper, plastic wrap, sharp knife, cutting board

1.	Dried apricots (about 40)	1½ cups	375 mL
	Water	1 tbsp.	15 mL
	Juice of 1 medium orange		
2.	Grated peel of 1 medium orange		
	Flake coconut	½ cup	125 mL
3.	Flake coconut	⅔ cup	150 mL

1. Measure the apricots and water into the casserole dish. Cover. Microwave on high (100%) for 2 minutes until moist and plump. Put the apricot mixture and orange juice into the blender. Place the lid on the blender. Process, stopping the blender and stirring every few seconds, until the apricots are very finely chopped (see Safety Tip, below). Put the apricot mixture into the bowl.

2. Mix in the orange peel and first amount of coconut. Divide the mixture in half. Roll into two 6 inch (15 cm) logs.

3. Place the second amount of coconut on the waxed paper. Roll the logs in the coconut until well coated. Cover each log with plastic wrap. Chill. Cut with the knife into 1 inch (2.5 cm) pieces on the cutting board. Makes 2 logs.

Pure and natural. All fruit and coconut.

Variation: Shape the mixture into 1 inch (2.5 cm) balls. Roll in the coconut. Chill. Makes about 18 balls.

Safety Tip: Follow manunfacturer's instructions for processing hot liquids.

Citrus Crunchies

GET READY ✔

measuring spoons, microwave-safe cup, dry measures, large bowl, mixing spoon

1.	Margarine	2 tbsp.	30 mL
2.	Rice squares cereal	3 cups	750 mL
	Package of lime, orange or grape-flavoured gelatin (jelly powder), about 3 tbsp., 50 mL	½ x 3 oz.	½ x 85 g

1. Microwave the margarine in the cup on high (100%) for 20 to 30 seconds until melted.

2. Measure the cereal into the bowl. Pour the melted margarine over the cereal. Toss with the mixing spoon until well coated. Sprinkle with the flavoured gelatin. Toss well. Microwave on high (100%) for 1 minute. Stir. Repeat 3 times. Makes 3 cups (750 mL) snack mix.

Great to have on hand for your lunch bag or as a dessert snack.

Corn Flakes Chews

GET READY ✔

liquid measures, large saucepan, long-handled mixing spoon, hot pad, measuring spoons, dry measures, waxed paper

1.	Liquid honey	¼ cup	60 mL
	Corn syrup	⅔ cup	150 mL
	Skim evaporated milk	¼ cup	60 mL
2.	Vanilla flavouring	1 tsp.	5 mL
	Corn flakes cereal	4 cups	1 L
	Fancy flake coconut	½ cup	125 mL

1. Combine the honey, corn syrup and evaporated milk in the saucepan. Heat on medium, stirring constantly with the mixing spoon, until the mixture starts to boil. Reduce the heat to medium-low. Simmer for 8 minutes. Do not stir. Remove the saucepan to the hot pad.

2. Add the vanilla, cereal and coconut. Mix well. Cool for 10 minutes. Drop by rounded tablespoonfuls onto the waxed paper. Grease your fingers. Shape into mounds. Chill for 30 minutes. Makes 24 chews.

Keep these chilled with your frozen drink box or lunch bag-size freezer pack —unless you like 'em sticky.

Banana Raisin Bars

GET READY ✔

9 × 13 inch (22 × 33 cm) oblong baking pan, dry measures, large bowl, mixing spoon, measuring spoons, small bowl, electric mixer, oven mitts, wire rack

1.			
	Quick-cooking rolled oats (not instant)	3 cups	750 mL
	Long thread coconut	1 cup	250 mL
	Raisins	1 cup	250 mL
	Sunflower seeds	½ cup	125 mL
	Peanuts, chopped	½ cup	125 mL
2.	Margarine	½ cup	125 mL
	Corn syrup	3 tbsp.	50 mL
	Liquid honey	3 tbsp.	50 mL
	Large egg	1	1
	Vanilla flavouring	1 tsp.	5 mL
	Mashed banana	⅓ cup	75 mL

1. Place the oven rack in the centre position. Turn the oven on to 325°F (160°C). Grease the baking pan. Combine the first 5 ingredients with the mixing spoon in the large bowl.

2. Beat the next 6 ingredients in the small bowl with the electric mixer on high speed until light and fluffy. Add the banana mixture to the rolled oat mixture. Combine well. Spread in the baking pan. Press down well with your hand. Bake in the oven for 50 minutes until firm and golden brown. Use the oven mitts to remove the baking pan to the wire rack. Cool. Cuts into 36 bars.

Pictured at right and on back cover.

Apple Raisin Bars: Substitute ½ cup (125 mL) applesauce for the banana and add ⅛ tsp. (0.5 mL) ground cinnamon.

Soft and chewy. These will remind you of banana bread.

Sweet Ending Pizza

GET READY ✔

12 inch (30 cm) pizza pan, dry measures, large bowl, electric mixer, measuring spoons, mixing spoon, oven mitts, hot pad, table knife

1.			
	Smooth peanut butter	¾ cup	175 mL
	Hard margarine, softened	½ cup	125 mL
	Brown sugar, packed	1 cup	250 mL
	Granulated sugar	¼ cup	60 mL
	Large eggs	2	2
	Vanilla flavouring	1 tsp.	5 mL
2.	All-purpose flour	1¾ cups	425 mL
	Baking soda	¾ tsp.	4 mL
	Baking powder	½ tsp.	2 mL
	Salt	½ tsp.	2 mL
3.	Semisweet chocolate chips	½ cup	125 mL
	Butterscotch chips	½ cup	125 mL
4.	Candy-coated chocolate candies	½ cup	125 mL

1. Place the oven rack in the centre position. Turn the oven on to 350°F (175°C). Grease the pizza pan. Cream the peanut butter and margarine together in the bowl with the electric mixer. Beat in both sugars. Beat in the eggs, 1 at a time. Add the vanilla. Stir with the mixing spoon.

2. Add the flour, baking soda, baking powder and salt. Stir just to moisten. Press in the pizza pan with your hand. Bake in the oven for 7 to 9 minutes until lightly browned. Use the oven mitts to remove the pan to the hot pad.

3. Sprinkle the hot pizza with both kinds of chips. Let stand to soften. Draw the knife back and forth to smooth out most of the chips.

4. Scatter the candies over the top of the chips. Lightly press the candies into the melted chips. Cool. Cuts into 16 wedges.

A soft peanut butter cookie crust.

Top: Iced Crispy Rice Squares, below
Centre: Simple Chocolate Fudge, page 63
Bottom: Butterscotch Bites, page 63

Iced Crispy Rice Squares

GET READY ✔

8 × 8 inch (20 × 20 cm) square baking pan, dry measures, large microwave-safe bowl, mixing spoon, 1 quart (1 L) casserole dish, table knife

1.	Large marshmallows	32	32
	Hard margarine	¼ cup	60 mL
2.	Crisp rice cereal	5 cups	1.25 L
3.	**CHOCOLATE PEANUT ICING**		
	Semisweet chocolate chips	1 cup	250 mL
	Smooth peanut butter	¼ cup	60 mL

1. Grease the baking pan. Put the marshmallows and margarine into the bowl. Microwave, uncovered, on high (100%) for about 2 minutes, stirring with the mixing spoon after 1 minute, until melted.

2. Add the cereal. Stir until well coated. Press in the pan with your hand. Cool until set.

3. **Chocolate Peanut Icing:** Put the chocolate chips and peanut butter into the casserole. Microwave, uncovered, on medium (50%) for about 2½ minutes, stirring at halftime, until melted and smooth. Spread with the knife on the squares. Cool until set. Cuts into 25 squares.

Simple Chocolate Fudge

GET READY ✔

8 × 8 inch (20 × 20 cm) square baking pan, dry measures, large microwave-safe bowl, mixing spoon

1.	Can of sweetened condensed milk	11 oz.	300 mL
	Semisweet chocolate chips	3 cups	750 mL
2.	Chopped walnuts	²/₃ cup	150 mL

1. Grease the baking pan. Put the condensed milk and chocolate chips into the bowl. Microwave, uncovered, on medium (50%) for about 2½ minutes, stirring often with the mixing spoon, until the chips are melted.

2. Add the walnuts. Stir. Spread in the pan. Chill. Cuts into 25 squares.

Pictured on page 62.

Butterscotch Bites

GET READY ✔

dry measures, liquid measures, large deep microwave-safe bowl, mixing spoon, baking sheet, waxed paper

1.	Granulated sugar	¾ cup	175 mL
	Hard margarine	¼ cup	60 mL
	Skim evaporated milk	⅓ cup	75 mL
2.	Butterscotch chips	½ cup	125 mL
3.	Quick-cooking rolled oats (not instant)	1¾ cups	425 mL
	Medium coconut	¼ cup	60 mL

1. Combine the sugar, margarine and evaporated milk with the mixing spoon in the bowl. Microwave, uncovered, on high (100%) for about 2 minutes until the mixture boils. Stir. Microwave on medium (50%) for 1 minute.

2. Add the chips. Stir until melted.

3. Mix in the rolled oats and coconut. Cover the baking sheet with the waxed paper. Drop the mixture by rounded tablespoonfuls onto the waxed paper. Chill until firm. Keep chilled. Makes about 2 dozen bites.

Pictured on page 62.

Your mouth will water for these.

Chocolate Chip Granola Bars

GET READY ✔

10 x 15 inch (25 x 38 cm) baking sheet, dry measures, liquid measures, large bowl, mixing spoon, waxed paper, oven mitts, wire rack

1.			
Rolled oats (not instant)	3 cups	750 mL
Flaked almonds	1 cup	250 mL
Shelled sunflower seeds	1 cup	250 mL
Raisins	1 cup	250 mL
Semisweet chocolate chips	1 cup	250 mL
Can of sweetened condensed milk	11 oz.	300 mL
Hard margarine, melted	¼ cup	60 mL

1. Place the oven rack in the centre position. Turn the oven on to 325°F (160°C). Grease the baking sheet. Combine all 7 ingredients with the mixing spoon in the bowl. The mixture will be stiff. Put into the baking sheet. Press down evenly with your hands using the waxed paper. Bake in the oven for 25 to 30 minutes until golden brown. Use the oven mitts to remove the baking sheet to the wire rack. Cool for 15 minutes. Cuts into 36 bars.

Pictured on page 9 and above.

Great any time of the day.

Puffed Wheat Candy Squares

GET READY ✓
dry measures, large bowl, 9 × 13 inch (22 × 33 cm) oblong baking pan, medium saucepan, liquid measures, measuring spoons, long-handled mixing spoon, hot pad

1.	Puffed wheat cereal	8 cups	2 L
2.	Hard margarine	⅓ cup	75 mL
	Golden corn syrup	½ cup	125 mL
	Liquid honey	1 tsp.	5 mL
	Smooth peanut butter	1½ tbsp.	25 mL
	Brown sugar, packed	1 cup	250 mL
3.	Vanilla flavouring	1 tsp.	5 mL
4.	Hard margarine	½ tsp.	2 mL

1. Measure the cereal into the bowl. Grease the pan.

2. Melt the first amount of margarine in the saucepan on medium. Add the corn syrup, honey, peanut butter and brown sugar. Heat on medium, stirring constantly with the mixing spoon, until the mixture comes to a boil and the brown sugar is dissolved. This should take about 30 to 40 seconds. Remove the saucepan to the hot pad.

3. Add the vanilla. Stir. Carefully pour the sauce over the cereal. Stir until the cereal is well coated. Put the cereal mixture into the pan.

4. Grease the palms of your hands with the second amount of margarine. Press the cereal mixture with your hand into the pan. Cool until set. Cuts into 48 squares.

Puffed Wheat Squares

GET READY ✔

9 x 9 inch (22 x 22 cm) square baking pan, dry measures, measuring spoons, medium saucepan, mixing spoon, hot pad, very large bowl, rubber spatula

1.	Hard margarine	⅓ cup	75 mL
	Light or dark corn syrup	½ cup	125 mL
	Brown sugar, packed	⅔ cup	150 mL
	Cocoa powder	2 tbsp.	30 mL
	Vanilla flavouring	1 tsp.	5 mL
2.	Puffed wheat cereal	8 cups	2 L

1. Grease the baking pan. Combine the margarine, corn syrup, brown sugar, cocoa powder and vanilla flavouring with the mixing spoon in the saucepan. Heat on medium, stirring constantly, until the mixture starts to boil with bubbles all over the surface. Remove the saucepan to the hot pad.

2. Measure the cereal into the bowl. Pour the hot chocolate mixture over the top. Use the rubber spatula to scrape the sides of the saucepan. Stir until well coated. Turn into the pan. Press down using the dampened spatula. Chill for about 2 hours to set. Cuts into 36 squares.

Pictured on page 67.

Crispy Rice Squares

GET READY ✔

9 × 9 inch (22 × 22 cm) square baking pan, dry measures, large saucepan (or Dutch oven), mixing spoon, hot pad, rubber spatula

1.	Hard margarine	¼ cup	60 mL
	Large marshmallows	36	36
2.	Crisp rice cereal	6 cups	1.5 L

1. Grease the pan. Put the margarine and marshmallows into the saucepan. Heat on medium, stirring often with the mixing spoon, until melted. Remove the saucepan to the hot pad.

2. Add the cereal. Stir until well coated. Scrape out all of the cereal into the pan. Press down firmly using the dampened rubber spatula. Chill for about 2 hours before cutting. Cuts into 36 squares.

Left: Puffed Wheat Squares, page 66
Right: Crispy Rice Squares, above

Very easy and quick to make. Spread as much liverwurst on the tortilla as you like.

"Wurst" Cheese & Lettuce Wrap

GET READY ✔

measuring spoons, table knife, dry measures, plastic wrap

1.			
Plain (or herbed) liverwurst	2-3 tbsp.	30-50 mL
White (or whole-wheat) flour tortilla (10 inch, 25 cm, size)	1	1
Grated Swiss cheese	⅓ cup	75 mL
Shredded lettuce	⅓-½ cup	75-125 mL

1. Spread the liverwurst with the knife on the tortilla. Sprinkle with the cheese and lettuce. Roll up tightly. Wrap with plastic wrap. Chill for at least 1 hour. Slice to serve. Makes 1 wrap.

Pictured on page 11 and above.

Vegetable Roll

measuring spoons, small bowl, mixing spoon, table knife, dry measures, plastic wrap

1.			
Plain spreadable cream cheese	1 tbsp.	15 mL
Ranch (or other creamy) dressing	1 tbsp.	15 mL
White (or whole-wheat) flour tortilla	1	1
(10 inch, 25 cm, size)		

2.			
Grated carrot	2 tbsp.	30 mL
Finely chopped green, red or	2 tbsp.	30 mL
yellow pepper		
Finely chopped green onion	2 tsp.	10 mL
Finely chopped broccoli florets	3 tbsp.	50 mL
Grated Cheddar cheese	¼ cup	60 mL

1. Combine the cream cheese and dressing with the mixing spoon in the bowl. Spread the cream cheese mixture with the knife on the tortilla.

2. Sprinkle the remaining 5 ingredients on the cream cheese mixture in the order given. Roll up tightly. Wrap with plastic wrap. Chill for at least 1 hour. Slice to serve. Makes 1 roll.

   Pictured at right and on front cover.

Bottom Left: Seeded Cheese (from After-School Snacks, page 90)
Top Right: Vegetable Roll, above

Try different flavoured dressings for a variety of tastes.

Roast Beef Rolls

GET READY ✔

measuring spoons, table knife, dry measures, plastic wrap

1.	Plain (or herbed) spreadable cream cheese	3 tbsp.	50 mL
	White (or whole wheat) flour tortilla (10 inch, 25 cm, size)	1	1
	Shredded lettuce	½ cup	125 mL
	Finely diced onion	1 tbsp.	15 mL
	Shaved roast beef (or 3 very thin slices)	2 oz.	57 g

1. Spread the cream cheese with the knife on the tortilla. Cover with the lettuce and onion. Lay the beef on top. Roll up tightly. Wrap with plastic wrap. Chill for at least 1 hour. Slice to serve. Makes 1 roll.

Try dipped in Honey Mustard Dunk, page 23.

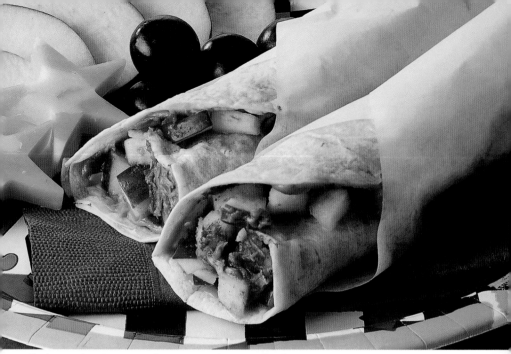

Much more fun than your ordinary peanut butter sandwich.

Peanut Butter Wrap

GET READY ✔

measuring spoons, table knife, dry measures, small cup, table spoon, plastic wrap

1.			
Peanut butter	2 tbsp.	30 mL
White (or whole-wheat) flour tortilla	1	1
(10 inch, 25 cm, size)		
Chopped apple, with peel	½ cup	125 mL
2.		
Brown sugar, packed	1 tsp.	5 mL
Ground cinnamon	¼ tsp.	1 mL

1. Spread the peanut butter with the knife on the tortilla. Scatter the apple on the peanut butter.

2. Combine the brown sugar and cinnamon with the spoon in the cup. Sprinkle over the apple. Roll up tightly. Wrap with plastic wrap. Chill for at least 1 hour. Makes 1 wrap.

Pack these for your lunch. Easy to eat.

Cucumber Under Wraps

GET READY ✔
measuring spoons, table knife, plastic wrap

1.	Plain (or herbed) spreadable cream cheese	½ cup	125 mL
	White (or whole-wheat) flour tortillas (8 inch, 20 cm, size)	4	4
2.	Cucumber piece (6 inches, 15 cm, long), quartered lengthwise	1	1
	Salt, sprinkle (optional)		
	Pepper, sprinkle (optional)		

1. Spread 2 tbsp. (30 mL) cream cheese with the knife on each tortilla.

2. Lay 1 cucumber spear on 1 edge of each tortilla. Sprinkle with the salt and pepper. Roll each tortilla around the cucumber. Wrap tightly with plastic wrap. Chill for at least 1 hour. Makes 4 wraps.

After-School Snacks

Lemon Cola Float

GET READY ✔
liquid measures, drinking glass, ice-cream scoop

1.	Cola soft drink, chilled	1 cup	250 mL
	Scoops of lemon sherbet	2	2

1. Pour the soft drink into the glass. Add the lemon sherbet. Makes 1 float.

The perfect beverage to treat yourself to after school.

Peach Melba Float

GET READY ✔
blender, 3 drinking glasses, liquid measures, mixing spoon, ice-cream scoop

1.	Can of sliced peaches, with juice	14 oz.	398 mL
2.	Ginger ale	2¼ cups	560 mL
3.	Scoops of raspberry sherbet 3		3

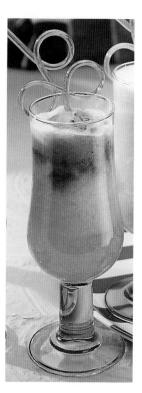

1. Put the peach slices into the blender. Place the lid on the blender. Process on high for 15 seconds or until smooth. Divide among the 3 glasses.

2. Pour ¾ cup (175 mL) ginger ale into each glass. Stir.

3. Add 1 scoop of the raspberry sherbet to each glass. Serve immediately. Makes 3 floats.

These flavours explode in your mouth.

Root Beer Float/Soda

GET READY ✓
ice-cream scoop, drinking glass, long-handled spoon

1. **Rounded scoops of vanilla ice cream**   2   2
    Chilled root beer, to fill the glass

1. Put the ice cream into the drinking glass.
    Pour the root beer over the ice cream to
    fill the glass. Makes 1 large drink.

Variation: Use any other flavour of your
favorite soft drink.

Whether you call this a float
or a soda, it is a cinch to
make any flavour you want.
Do not freeze.

Banana Berry Yogurt Shake

GET READY ✔

dry measures, liquid measures, blender

1.			
	Plain yogurt	1 cup	250 mL
	Liquid or creamed honey	¼ cup	60 mL
	Banana	1	1
	Prepared orange juice	½ cup	125 mL
2.	Large frozen strawberries	6	6

1. Put the first 4 ingredients into the blender. Place the lid on the blender. Process for 30 seconds or until the banana is smooth.

2. While the blender is processing, add the strawberries, 1 at a time, through the opening in the lid. Process until smooth. Makes 1 large shake.

This makes a nice breakfast drink too.

Great for a cold winter warm-up after school.

Hot Chocolate For One

GET READY ✔

measuring spoons, 12 oz. (341 mL) microwave-safe mug, liquid measures, mixing spoon

1.	Cocoa powder	1 tbsp.	15 mL
	Granulated sugar	1 tbsp.	15 mL
2.	Water	¾ cup	175 mL
3.	Skim evaporated milk	⅔ cup	150 mL
4.	Vanilla flavouring	¾ tsp.	4 mL
	Miniature marshmallows, for garnish		

1. Combine the cocoa powder and sugar in the mug.

2. Put the water in the 1 cup (250 mL) liquid measure. Microwave on high (100%) for 1½ minutes or until it boils. Pour the hot water slowly into the cocoa mixture. Stir until smooth.

3. Pour the evaporated milk into the same liquid measure. Microwave on high (100%) for 1 minute. Pour the warm milk into the mug.

4. Add the vanilla. Stir well. Place the marshmallows on top. Serves 1.

Strawberry Pineapple Cooler

GET READY ✔
liquid measures, measuring spoons, blender, mixing spoon

1. Pineapple juice, chilled	1 cup	250 mL
Skim milk powder	2 tbsp.	30 mL
Large frozen strawberries	3	3
2. Ginger ale (or club soda), optional	½ cup	125 mL

1. Combine the pineapple juice and milk powder in the blender. Place the lid on the blender. Process for 10 seconds. While the blender is processing, add the strawberries, 1 at a time, through the opening in the lid. Process until smooth.

2. Add the ginger ale to have a fizzy cooler. Stir. Makes 1⅓ cups (325 mL).

BLUEBERRY PINEAPPLE COOLER: Follow the directions as above, substituting ½ cup (125 mL) frozen blueberries for the strawberries.

A lovely deep mauve with a light mauve foam on top. The soft drink adds a little fizz.

Add a selection of veggies to round out a healthy snack.

Dill Dip

GET READY ✔

dry measures, measuring spoons, small bowl, mixing spoon

1.	Salad dressing (or mayonnaise)	⅔ cup	150 mL
	Sour cream	⅔ cup	150 mL
	Onion flakes	2 tsp.	10 mL
	Parsley flakes	2 tsp.	10 mL
	Dill weed	2 tsp.	10 mL
	Paprika	¼ tsp.	1 mL
	Celery salt	¼ tsp.	1 mL

1. Combine all 7 ingredients in the bowl. Mix well. Makes about 1½ cups (375 mL) dip.

Spread on bread, bagels or crackers. Store any remaining spread in a covered container in the refrigerator for up to three days.

Smoked Salmon Spread

GET READY ✔

small bowl, table fork, dry measures, measuring spoons, mixing spoon

1.	Can of salmon, well drained	7½ oz.	213 g
	Plain spreadable cream cheese	⅓ cup	75 mL
	Finely chopped celery	1 tbsp.	15 mL
	Prepared horseradish	½ tsp.	2 mL
	Liquid smoke flavouring	⅛ tsp.	0.5 mL
	Onion powder	⅛ tsp.	0.5 mL

1. Mash the salmon in the bowl with the fork. Add the remaining 5 ingredients. Mix well. Makes 1 cup (250 mL) spread.

Spread on graham crackers, digestive biscuits or any other whole-wheat or whole grain cracker.

Choco-Nut Spread

GET READY ✔

dry measures, liquid measures, measuring spoons, small bowl, mixing spoon

1.	Smooth peanut butter	½ cup	125 mL
	Chocolate syrup	⅓ cup	75 mL
	Vanilla flavouring	1 tsp.	5 mL

1. Combine all 3 ingredients in the bowl. Mix until smooth. Makes ¾ cup (175 mL) spread.

Taffy Fruit Dip

GET READY ✔

dry measures, measuring spoons, medium bowl, electric mixer, mixing spoon

1.	Cream cheese, softened	4 oz.	125 g
	Brown sugar, packed	½ cup	125 mL
	Vanilla flavouring	2 tsp.	10 mL
2.	Chopped peanuts (optional)	¼ cup	60 mL
	Fresh fruit, for dipping		

1. Beat the first 3 ingredients in the bowl with the mixer on medium speed until smooth and fluffy and the brown sugar is dissolved.

2. Stir in the peanuts. Dip the fresh fruit into the taffy dip. Chill any remaining dip. It will stiffen slightly. Soften in the microwave oven on low (20%) for just a few seconds. Makes ¾ cup (175 mL) dip.

Pictured on page 83.

Honey Lime Fruit Dip

GET READY ✔

dry measures, measuring spoons, small bowl, mixing spoon

1.	Sour cream (or thick plain yogurt)	1 cup	250 mL
	Liquid honey	2 tbsp.	30 mL
	Grated peel and juice of 1 medium lime		
	Poppy seeds (optional)	½ tsp.	2 mL

1. Combine all 4 ingredients in the bowl. Mix well. Chill for 5 minutes to blend the flavours. Makes 1 cup (250 mL) dip.

Pictured on page 83.

Clockwise From Top Right: Taffy Fruit Dip, page 82; Honey Lime Fruit Dip, page 82
Honey Mustard Dip, below

Honey Mustard Dip

GET READY ✓

dry measures, measuring spoons, small bowl, mixing spoon

1.	Sour cream	½ cup	125 mL
	Liquid honey	1 tbsp.	15 mL
	Prepared mustard	2 tsp.	10 mL

1. Combine all 3 ingredients in the bowl. Mix well. Makes ½ cup (125 mL) dip.

This will become a favorite in your home.

Whole-Wheat Bonkers Bread

GET READY ✔

12 inch (30 cm) pizza pan or 10 × 15 inch (25 × 38 cm) baking sheet, measuring spoons, dry measures, 2 small bowls, mixing spoon, liquid measures, medium bowl, whisk, tea towel, sharp knife, pastry brush, oven mitts, wire rack

1.	Instant yeast	1 tbsp.	15 mL
	Whole-wheat flour	1 cup	250 mL
2.	Very warm water	1 cup	250 mL
	Cooking oil	1 tbsp.	15 mL
	Granulated sugar	1 tsp.	5 mL
	Salt	1 tsp.	5 mL
3.	All-purpose flour	1½ cups	375 mL
4.	Hard margarine, melted	2 tbsp.	30 mL
	Garlic powder	⅛ tsp.	0.5 mL
	Dried sweet basil	1 tsp.	5 mL
5.	Grated Parmesan cheese	2 tbsp.	30 mL

1. Place the oven rack in the centre position. Turn the oven on to 400°F (205°C). Grease the pan. Combine the yeast and whole-wheat flour in the first small bowl. Set aside.

2. Combine the water, cooking oil, sugar and salt in the medium bowl. Stir until dissolved. Add the whole-wheat flour mixture. Whisk until smooth.

3. Add the all-purpose flour. Mix well. Cover the bowl with the tea towel. Let stand for 15 minutes.

4. Combine the margarine, garlic powder and basil in the second small bowl. Knead the flour mixture 3 or 4 times. Press out evenly in the greased pan. Cut into 14 sticks or fingers with the sharp knife. Brush the margarine mixture over the surface of the dough.

5. Sprinkle with the Parmesan cheese. Cover the baking sheet with the tea towel. Let stand for 15 minutes. Bake, uncovered, in the oven for 20 minutes or until lightly golden. Use the oven mitts to remove the pan to the wire rack to cool. Makes 14 bread sticks.

Crunchy Maple Yogurt

GET READY ✔

dry measures, medium microwave-safe bowl, waxed paper, 2 mixing spoons, oven mitts, hot pad, measuring spoons, small bowl, 2 dessert bowls, covered container

1. CRUMBLE TOPPING

Hard margarine	¼ cup	60 mL
Rolled oats (not instant)	¾ cup	175 mL
Brown sugar, packed	¼ cup	60 mL
Graham cracker crumbs	¼ cup	60 mL
Long thread or fancy flake coconut	¼ cup	60 mL

2. MAPLE YOGURT

Plain yogurt	8 oz.	250 g
Liquid honey	2 tsp.	10 mL
Maple flavouring	¼ tsp.	1 mL

1. **Crumble Topping:** Put the margarine into the microwave-safe bowl. Cover with the waxed paper. Microwave on high (100%) for 30 seconds. Add the next 4 ingredients. Mix well. Microwave on high (100%) for 30 seconds or until nicely toasted. Use the oven mitts to remove the bowl to the hot pad. Break up the mixture as it cools.

2. **Maple Yogurt:** Mix all 3 ingredients in the small bowl. Divide between the 2 dessert bowls and sprinkle each with the Crumble Topping. Store any remaining topping in a covered container in the refrigerator. Serves 2.

Crumble Topping is great to sprinkle over yogurt, fruit or pudding.

Fruity Chicken Pitas

GET READY ✔

dry measures, medium bowl, mixing spoon, measuring spoons, small bowl, rubber spatula, sharp knife, table spoon

1.	Diced cooked chicken (or turkey)	1 cup	250 mL
	Small apple, cored and diced	1	1
	Can of pineapple tidbits, well drained	8 oz.	227 mL
	Crushed potato chips	1 cup	250 mL
2.	Salad dressing (or mayonnaise)	½ cup	125 mL
	Raisins	5 tbsp.	75 mL
	Ground cinnamon	¼ tsp.	1 mL
	Chopped walnuts (optional)	2 tbsp.	30 mL
3.	Mini pita breads	10	10

1. Combine the first 4 ingredients in the medium bowl. Stir.

2. Combine the next 4 ingredients in the small bowl. Stir. Fold the salad dressing mixture into the chicken mixture with the rubber spatula until coated.

3. Carefully slit each pita bread open at one end with the knife. Fill each pita "pocket" with ¼ cup (60 mL) mixture. Makes 2½ cups (625 mL), enough for 10 pitas.

Store leftover filling in the refrigerator for 2 to 3 days.

Salad Envelopes

GET READY ✔

sharp knife, cutting board, paper towel, table spoon, dry measures, medium bowl, mixing spoon, measuring spoons, 2 paper towels

1.	**Medium tomato**	**1**	**1**
2.	**Grated carrot**	**¼ cup**	**60 mL**
	Green onion, thinly sliced	**1**	**1**
	Thinly sliced green, red or yellow pepper (2 inches, 5 cm, long)	**¼ cup**	**60 mL**
	Grated Cheddar cheese	**1 cup**	**250 mL**
3.	**Creamy dressing (your favorite)**	**2 tbsp.**	**30 mL**
	Shredded iceberg lettuce	**⅔ cup**	**150 mL**
	White (or whole-wheat) flour tortillas (10 inch, 25 cm, size)	**2**	**2**

1. Cut the tomato in half with the knife on the cutting board. Gently squeeze over the paper towel to remove the seeds. Use the table spoon to scoop out the rest. Throw away the seeds and juice. Dice the tomato into 1 inch (2.5 cm) chunks on the cutting board.

2. Combine the tomato with the carrot, green onion, green pepper and cheese in the bowl. Stir.

3. Add the dressing. Toss the mixture to coat. Spread ½ of the lettuce down the middle of each tortilla. Spread ½ of the veggie mixture over the lettuce. Fold the bottom edge of the tortilla up over the filling to the centre. Fold the left side over the centre. Fold the right side overlapping the left side. Wrap in the paper towels to eat. Makes 2 envelopes.

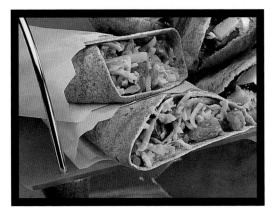

A salad you can eat with your fingers.

Great for a fast after-school snack.

Peanut Butter Log

GET READY ✔

measuring spoons, small bowl, mixing spoon, table knife, waxed paper

1.	Smooth or chunky peanut butter	2 tbsp.	30 mL
	Cream cheese, softened (or spreadable fruit-flavoured cream cheese)	1 tbsp.	15 mL
2.	White (or whole-wheat) flour tortilla (10 inch, 25 cm, size)	1	1
3.	Medium carrot, grated	1	1
	Light raisins	2 tbsp.	30 mL

1. Use the spoon to cream the peanut butter and cream cheese together in the bowl.

2. Use the knife to spread the peanut butter mixture on one side of the tortilla.

3. Sprinkle the carrot and raisins over the peanut butter. Press down with your hand. Roll the tortilla up like a jelly roll. Wrap one end with the waxed paper and eat with your hands. Makes 1 log.

Fruit Roll Tortillas

GET READY ✔
small bowl, table fork, measuring spoons, dry measures, mixing spoon, table knife, plastic wrap

1.	Cream cheese, softened	4 oz.	125 g
2.	Icing (confectioner's) sugar	2 tbsp.	30 mL
	Can of crushed pineapple, well drained (see Tip)	8 oz.	227 mL
	Long thread coconut	¼ cup	60 mL
3.	White (or whole-wheat) flour tortillas (10 inch, 25 cm, size)	3	3

1. Put the cream cheese into the bowl. Use the fork to mash the cream cheese until smooth.

2. Add the icing sugar, pineapple and coconut. Mix well.

3. Divide the mixture among the tortillas. Spread with the knife. Roll each tortilla up like a jelly roll. Cover with plastic wrap. Chill for at least 1 hour. Cuts into 30, 1 inch (2.5 cm) pinwheels or 3 whole rolls.

Tip: Save the pineapple juice, chill and top up with some ginger ale and a cherry for a great beverage treat!

These will keep for several days in the fridge. Eat sliced or leave whole.

Seeded Cheese

GET READY ✔

measuring spoons, pie plate, oven mitts, wire rack, microwave-safe plate

1.	Sesame seeds	2 tbsp.	30 mL
2.	Cheese (your favorite), cut into 10 sticks, ½ inch (12 mm) thick, ½ inch (12 mm) wide and about 3 inches (7 cm) long	6 oz.	170 g

1. Place the oven rack in the upper position (second from the top). Turn the oven on to broil. Place the sesame seeds in the ungreased pie plate. Broil the seeds in the oven for about 3 minutes, shaking the pie plate occasionally, using the oven mitts, until the seeds are golden brown. Use the oven mitts to remove the pie plate to the wire rack. Cool slightly.

2. Place the cheese on the microwave-safe plate. Microwave, uncovered, on high (100%) for 6 seconds until warm. Lightly press and roll the warmed cheese sticks in the seeds. Chill for 30 minutes. Makes about 10 cheese sticks.

   Pictured on front cover, on page 69, on page 73 and at right.

Cheese lovers will devour these!

This is worth hurrying home from school to make. Recipe may be halved if desired. Do not freeze.

Nacho Two Step

GET READY ✔

cookie sheet, sharp knife, cutting board, paper towel, table spoon, medium bowl, dry measures, measuring spoons, mixing spoon, oven mitts, wire rack

1.	Bag of tortilla chips	8 oz.	225 g
2.	Medium tomatoes	2	2
	Can of diced green chilies, drained	4 oz.	114 mL
	Sliced green onion	¼ cup	60 mL
	Chili powder	½ tsp.	2 mL
	Grated mild or medium Cheddar cheese	¼ cup	60 mL
3.	Grated Monterey Jack cheese	2 cups	500 mL

1. Place the rack in the centre position in the oven. Turn the oven on to 350°F (175°C). Pour the tortilla chips onto the cookie sheet. Crowd them together so not much of the cookie sheet shows underneath.

2. Cut the tomatoes in half with the knife on the cutting board. Gently squeeze each half over the paper towel to remove the seeds. Use the table spoon to scoop out the rest. Throw away the seeds. Dice the tomato on the cutting board. Put into the bowl. Add the green chilies, green onion, chili powder and Cheddar cheese. Stir. Spoon over the chips.

3. Sprinkle the Monterey Jack cheese over the top. Bake in the oven for about 10 minutes until the cheese is melted. Use the oven mitts to remove the cookie sheet to the wire rack. Serves 2.

Left: Stuffed Pita, below Right: Piece O'Pizza, page 93

Stuffed Pita

GET READY ✔

dry measures, measuring spoons, medium bowl, mixing spoon, table spoon, paper towel, microwave-safe plate

1.	Medium pita bread, cut in half	1	1
	Mozzarella cheese slices	4	4
2.	Cooked ham slices, slivered	2	2
	Small tomato, diced and drained	1	1
	Thinly sliced celery	¼ cup	60 mL
	Seeded and grated cucumber, drained	½ cup	125 mL
	Slivered red pepper	3 tbsp.	50 mL
	Sweet pickle relish	2 tsp.	10 mL
	Chopped iceberg lettuce	1 cup	250 mL
	Salad dressing (or mayonnaise)	1 tbsp.	15 mL
3.	Alfalfa sprouts (optional)	½ cup	125 mL

1. Line each pita half with 2 slices of the cheese.

2. Mix the next 8 ingredients in the bowl. Spoon the mixture into the centre of the pitas between the cheese slices. Arrange on the paper towel on the plate. Microwave on high (100%) for 1 to 2 minutes until the cheese melts.

3. Tuck the alfalfa sprouts around the top edges. Makes 2 servings.

Piece O'Pizza

GET READY ✔

dry measures, measuring spoons, 3 quart (3 L) casserole dish, mixing spoon,
liquid measures, table knife, paper towel

1.	Lean ground beef	1 lb.	454 g
	Chopped onion	1 cup	250 mL
	Medium green pepper, chopped	1	1
	Grated carrot	½ cup	125 mL
	Salt	1½ tsp.	7 mL
2.	Pizza sauce	1¼ cups	300 mL
	Can of mushroom pieces, drained	10 oz.	284 mL
3.	English muffins, split	3	3
	Pimiento-stuffed olives, sliced	18	18
	Grated medium Cheddar cheese	6 tbsp.	100 mL
	Grated mozzarella cheese	6 tbsp.	100 mL

1. Combine the first 5 ingredients in the casserole dish. Crumble together. Cover. Microwave on high (100%) for about 10 minutes, stirring at halftime, until no pink remains in the beef and vegetables are cooked.

2. Add the pizza sauce and mushrooms. Stir. Makes 5 cups (1.25 L).

3. Use the knife to spread 2 tbsp. (30 mL) beef mixture over each muffin half. Lay the slices of olives over each, followed by 1 tbsp. (15 mL) of each cheese. Arrange in a circle on the paper towel in the microwave. Microwave, uncovered, on high (100%) for about 55 seconds for each muffin half, rotating ½ turn at halftime if you don't have a turntable, until the cheese is melted. Allow 3 minutes for 6 muffin halves if done together. Freeze remaining beef mixture or make more pizzas. Makes 6 pizza muffins.

Pictured on page 92.

Vegetable Pizza

GET READY ✔

12 inch (30 cm) pizza pan, dry measures, liquid measures, small bowl, mixing spoon, oven mitts, wire rack, table knife, measuring spoons

1.	Biscuit mix	1⅛ cups	280 mL
	Milk	¼ cup	60 mL
2.	Spaghetti sauce	¼ cup	60 mL
3.	Grated mozzarella cheese	1 cup	250 mL
	Chopped green pepper	2 tbsp.	30 mL
	Sliced fresh mushrooms	¼ cup	60 mL
	Finely chopped onion	2 tbsp.	30 mL
	Pitted ripe olives, sliced	5-6	5-6

1. Place the oven rack in the centre position. Turn the oven on to 375°F (190°C). Grease the pizza pan. Mix the biscuit mix and milk in the bowl to make a soft dough. Press firmly on the pan with your hand. Bake in the oven for 15 minutes to partially cook. Use the oven mitts to remove the pizza pan to the wire rack.

2. Use the knife to spread the spaghetti sauce over the crust.

3. Sprinkle the cheese over the top. Sprinkle with the green pepper, mushrooms, onion and olives. Bake in the oven for about 15 minutes until the cheese has bubbled up through the toppings. Use the oven mitts to remove the pizza pan to the wire rack. Cuts into 6 wedges.

Make as cheesy as you like just by adding more or less cheese. You can also add more or less of your favorite toppings, too.

Made with English muffins, these are quick and easy to make. Sure to become a real hit.

Mock Pizza

GET READY ✔

baking sheet, measuring spoons, small bowl, mixing spoon, table knife, dry measures, oven mitts, wire rack

1.	English muffins, cut in half	6	6
2.	Can of tomato sauce	7½ oz.	213 mL
	Dried sweet basil	¼ tsp.	1 mL
	Ground oregano	¼ tsp.	1 mL
	Onion powder	¼ tsp.	1 mL
	Parsley flakes	¼ tsp.	1 mL
	Seasoned salt	½ tsp.	2 mL
3.	Grated mozzarella cheese	1 cup	250 mL
	Cherry tomatoes, sliced	12	12
	Small fresh mushrooms, sliced	12	12
	Bite-size pepperoni pieces	60	60
4.	Grated mozzarella cheese	⅓ cup	75 mL

1. Place the oven rack in the top position. Turn the oven on to broil. Arrange the muffin halves on the ungreased baking sheet.

2. Stir the next 6 ingredients in the bowl. Divide and spread the mixture over the muffin halves with the knife.

3. Layer the next 4 ingredients over the tomato sauce in the order given.

4. Sprinkle the second amount of cheese over the pepperoni. Heat under the broiler until the cheese is melted and bubbly. Use the oven mitts to remove the baking sheet to the wire rack. Serves 4.

Tomato Mozza Rounds

GET READY ✔

measuring spoons, small bowl, mixing spoon, baking sheet, oven mitts, wire rack, pancake lifter, table spoon, dry measures

1.	**Medium tomato, chopped**	1	1
	Olive oil	1 tbsp.	15 mL
	Garlic powder	⅛ tsp.	0.5 mL
	Salt	¼ tsp.	1 mL
	Grated Parmesan cheese	2 tsp.	10 mL
	Dried sweet basil	1 tsp.	5 mL
2.	**French bread slices (cut 1 inch, 2.5 cm, thick)**	2	2
3.	**Grated mozzarella cheese**	¼ cup	60 mL
	Pitted ripe olives, sliced (optional)		

1. Place the rack in the oven in the top position. Turn the oven on to broil. Combine the first 6 ingredients in the bowl. Mix well.

2. Place the bread slices on the ungreased baking sheet. Heat under the broiler until browned. Use the oven mitts to remove the baking sheet to the wire rack to cool slightly. Turn the bread over with the pancake lifter. Spoon the tomato mixture on the untoasted side of the bread.

3. Sprinkle with the cheese and olives. Heat under the broiler until the cheese is melted. Use the oven mitts to remove the baking sheet to the wire rack. Let stand for 1 minute. Makes 2 large rounds.

A kid's type bruschetta (pronounced broo-SKET-ah).

Cracker Nachos

GET READY ✔
9 × 9 inch (22 × 22 cm) square baking pan, dry measures, measuring spoons, oven mitts, wire rack

1.	Woven wheat crackers (such as Triscuit)	20	20
2.	Grated Cheddar cheese	½ cup	125 mL
	Green onions, sliced	2	2
	Medium green pepper, finely chopped	½	½
	Imitation bacon bits (or crisp cooked bacon, crumbled)	2 tbsp.	30 mL
	Grated Cheddar cheese	½ cup	125 mL
3.	Salsa (optional)		

1. Place the oven rack in the centre position. Turn the oven on to 350°F (175°C). Place the crackers close together in the ungreased pan.

2. Sprinkle the first amount of cheese, green onion, green pepper and bacon bits over top of the crackers. Sprinkle with the second amount of cheese. Bake, uncovered, in the oven for 15 minutes. Use the oven mitts to remove the pan to the wire rack.

3. Spoon the salsa on top. Serves 4.

A very easy whole-wheat version of nachos.

Pita Pizzas

GET READY ✓

measuring spoons, table knife, dry measures, baking sheet, oven mitts, wire rack

1.	Pita breads	2	2
	Pizza sauce	3 tbsp.	50 mL
2.	Any combination to make (chopped fresh mushrooms, chopped green pepper, chopped tomato, chopped green onion, pineapple tidbits, cooked crumbled bacon, deli meat such as ham or pepperoni)	⅔ cup	150 mL
3.	Grated mozzarella cheese	½ cup	125 mL

1. Place the oven rack in the centre position. Turn the oven on to broil. Spread each pita with 1½ tbsp. (25 mL) sauce with the knife, spreading to the edges.

2. Sprinkle 1 pita with ½ of the toppings. Repeat.

3. Sprinkle the cheese over the toppings. Lay the pitas on the ungreased baking sheet. Heat under the broiler for 8 to 9 minutes until the cheese is melted and the edges are crispy. Use the oven mitts to remove the baking sheet to the wire rack. Makes 2 pita pizzas.

These pizzas can be assembled and frozen before baking. When those hunger pangs hit, pop the frozen pizza in the oven and broil for eight to nine minutes.

The chunkier the salsa, the better! Serve with a dollop of sour cream.

Quesadillas

GET READY ✓

baking sheet, dry measures, table knife, pancake lifter, oven mitts, wire rack

1.	White (or whole-wheat) flour tortilla (10 inch, 25 cm, size)	1	1
2.	Chunky salsa	⅓ cup	75 mL
	Grated Cheddar cheese	⅓ cup	75 mL

1. Place the oven rack in the centre position. Turn the oven on to 400°F (205°C). Lay the tortilla out flat on the ungreased baking sheet.

2. Use the knife to spread the salsa on ½ of the tortilla. Sprinkle with the cheese. Fold the other ½ of the tortilla over top of the cheese. Press down lightly with your hand. Bake in the oven for 4 minutes. Use the pancake lifter to turn the quesadilla over. Bake for 4 minutes. Use the oven mitts to remove the baking sheet to the wire rack. Cool slightly. Cuts into 3 wedges.

This tuna sandwich is warmed in the oven and makes a nice warm treat on a chilly day.

Toasty Tuna Torpedoes

GET READY ✔

dry measures, measuring spoons, medium bowl, mixing spoon, sharp knife, cutting board, 4 large pieces of foil, oven mitts, 4 small plates

1.	Can of tuna, drained and flaked	6½ oz.	184 g
	Grated Cheddar cheese	1 cup	250 mL
	Chopped dill pickle	2 tbsp.	30 mL
	Green onion, thinly sliced	1	1
2.	Prepared mustard	1 tbsp.	15 mL
	Salad dressing (or mayonnaise)	1 tbsp.	15 mL
3.	Hot dog buns	4	4

1. Place the oven rack in the centre position. Turn the oven on to 350°F (175°C). Combine the tuna, cheese, pickle and green onion in the bowl. Stir.

2. Add the mustard and salad dressing. Stir.

3. Cut the hot dog buns horizontally with the knife on the cutting board, making sure to not cut all the way through. Open the buns and stuff with the tuna mixture. Wrap in the foil. Bake in the oven for 15 minutes. Use the oven mitts to remove the sandwiches to the plates. Cool each sandwich slightly before unwrapping. Makes 4 torpedoes.

Bean Quesadillas

GET READY ✔

baking sheet, dry measures, table knife, sharp knife, cutting board, paper towel, table spoon, oven mitts, wire rack

1.	White (or whole-wheat) flour tortilla (10 inch, 25 cm, size)	1	1
2.	Refried beans with green chilies	⅓ cup	75 mL
3.	Small tomato	1	1
	Grated Cheddar cheese	½ cup	125 mL

1. Place the oven rack in the centre position. Turn the oven on to 400°F (205°C). Lay the tortilla out flat on the ungreased baking sheet.

2. Spread the beans over the tortilla with the table knife.

3. Cut the tomato in half with the sharp knife on the cutting board. Gently squeeze over the paper towel to remove the seeds. Use the table spoon to scoop out the rest. Throw away the seeds and juice. Dice the tomato into small chunks on the cutting board. Sprinkle the tomato and cheese over ½ of the beans. Fold the plain bean half over the bean, tomato and cheese half. Press down lightly with your hand. Bake in the oven for 10 minutes. Use the oven mitts to remove the baking sheet to the wire rack. Let stand for 3 to 5 minutes before cutting. Cuts into 6 wedges.

Macaroni Magic

GET READY ✔

large saucepan, dry measures, mixing spoon, 8 inch (20 cm) casserole dish, sharp knife, cutting board, paper towel, table spoon, small bowl, measuring spoons, oven mitts, wire rack

1.	Package of macaroni and cheese dinner	6½ oz.	200 g
	Chopped onion	¾ cup	175 mL
2.	Can of sliced mushrooms, drained	10 oz.	284 mL
	Can of flaked chicken	6½ oz.	184 g
3.	Large tomato	1	1
	Dried sweet basil	1 tsp.	5 mL
	Granulated sugar	¼ tsp.	1 mL
	Salt, light sprinkle		
	Pepper, light sprinkle		

1. Place the oven rack in the centre position. Turn the oven on to 350°F (175°C). Prepare the macaroni and cheese in the saucepan as the package directs, adding the onion before cooking.

2. Stir the mushrooms and chicken into the prepared macaroni. Turn into the casserole dish.

3. Cut the tomato in half with the knife on the cutting board. Gently squeeze over the paper towel to remove the seeds. Use the table spoon to scoop out the rest. Throw away the seeds and juice. Chop the tomato on the cutting board. Put into the bowl. Add the basil and sugar. Stir. Sprinkle with the salt and pepper. Stir. Pile on the centre of the casserole. Cover. Bake in the oven for 20 to 30 minutes until heated through. Use the oven mitts to remove the casserole dish to the wire rack. Serves 4.

Pictured on page 103.

Bologna Cups, below, make a wonderful container to fill with Macaroni Magic, page 102.

Bologna Cups

GET READY ✔
frying pan, table fork

1.	**Bologna slices**	4	4

1. Fry the bologna in the frying pan for about 2 minutes. They will puff up in the centre. Do not flatten. Turn the slices over with the fork. Fry for about 1 minute. Turn the "cups" right side up. Makes 4.

These are great warm or cold.

Ham & Cheese Delights

GET READY ✔

measuring spoons, medium bowl, mixing spoon, table knife, baking sheet, oven mitts, wire rack

1.	Cream cheese, softened	8 oz.	250 g
	Sweet pickle relish	1½ tbsp.	25 mL
	Ham slices, diced	5	5
	Onion powder	¼ tsp.	1 mL
2.	Refrigerator crescent-style rolls (tube of 8)	8½ oz.	235 g

1. Place the oven rack in the centre position. Turn the oven on to 375°F (190°C). Combine the cream cheese, relish, ham and onion powder in the bowl. Mix well.

2. Open the crescent roll tube and separate the rolls into 8 triangles. Use the knife to spread 2 tbsp. (30 mL) ham mixture on each triangle. Roll from the shortest side of the triangle to the opposite point. Place the rolls on the ungreased baking sheet. Bake in the oven for 12 minutes until golden brown. Use the oven mitts to remove the baking sheet to the wire rack. Makes 8 "delights."

Corn Doggies

GET READY ✓

medium bowl, dry measures, measuring spoons, mixing spoon, table fork, rolling pin, ruler, table knife, baking sheet, pastry brush, oven mitts, wire rack

1.			
Envelope of pie crust mix	9½ oz.	270 g
Yellow cornmeal	⅓ cup	75 mL
Chili powder	1 tsp.	5 mL
Cold water, approximately	6 tbsp.	100 mL
All-purpose flour, as needed, to prevent sticking when rolling		
2.	Wieners	8	8
	Large egg, fork-beaten	1	1

1. Place the oven rack in the centre position. Turn the oven on to 450°F (230°C). Pour the pie crust mix into the bowl. Stir in the cornmeal and chili powder. Slowly add the cold water, 1 tbsp. (15 mL) at a time, stirring with the fork after each addition. The dough should start to pull away from the sides of the bowl and form a ball. Divide in half. Roll each half into a 5 × 12 inch (12.5 × 30 cm) rectangle on a lightly floured counter or working surface. Cut each rectangle crosswise into 4 equal rectangles.

2. Place a wiener lengthwise across each rectangle. Brush the egg on 1 of the long edges of the pastry. Bring the 2 long edges of the rectangle up over the wiener and press together to seal. Place, seam-side down, on the ungreased baking sheet. Repeat with each rectangle. Brush the remaining egg on each surface. Bake in the oven for 12 minutes until crisp and golden brown. Use the oven mitts to remove the baking sheet to the wire rack. Makes 8 wrapped wieners.

    Pictured on page 99 and at right.

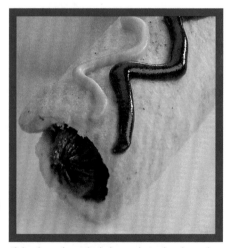

Make these the night before and simply reheat when you get home from school. These also freeze well.

Pizza Sticks

GET READY ✔

baking sheet, dry measures, measuring spoons, large bowl, mixing spoon, liquid measures, rolling pin, ruler, sharp knife, cutting board, tea towel, small cup, pastry brush, oven mitts, wire rack

1.			
All-purpose flour	2 cups	500 mL
Salt	½ tsp.	2 mL
Granulated sugar	¼ tsp.	1 mL
Dried sweet basil	½ tsp.	2 mL
Instant yeast	1 tbsp.	15 mL
Olive (or cooking) oil	1½ tbsp.	25 mL
Hot water	1 cup	250 mL
All-purpose flour, approximately	½ cup	125 mL
Chopped pepperoni	⅔ cup	150 mL
2. Hard margarine, melted	2 tbsp.	30 mL
Garlic powder	¼ tsp.	1 mL

1. Place the oven rack in the centre position. Grease the baking sheet. Stir the first 5 ingredients together in the bowl. Pour in the olive oil and hot water. Stir until the flour is combined. Work in the second amount of flour until the dough is no longer sticky. Turn out onto a lightly floured surface. Knead for about 5 minutes, adding more flour as needed and a bit of the chopped pepperoni, until all the pepperoni is mixed into the dough. Invert the bowl over the dough. Let the dough rest for 10 minutes. Roll the dough out to about ½ inch (12 mm) thick. Cut rows about 1 inch (2.5 cm) wide with the knife on the cutting board. Cut crosswise into 5 inch (12.5 cm) sticks. Lay each stick on the baking sheet, about 2 inches (5 cm) apart. Cover with the tea towel. Let rise in the oven, with the door closed and the oven light on, for 30 minutes.

2. Remove the baking sheet from the oven. Turn the oven on to 375°F (190°C). Combine the melted margarine and garlic powder in the cup. Brush the sticks with the margarine mixture. Bake in the oven for 20 minutes. Use the oven mitts to remove the baking sheet to the wire rack. Makes 18 to 20 sticks.

Pictured on page 107 and on back cover.

Slightly crusty golden strips of bread. Specks of pepperoni throughout. Nippy taste.

Kid Kabobs

GET READY ✔
4 inch (10 cm) wooden bamboo skewer, small microwave-safe plate

1.	Wiener pieces (1 wiener)	3	3
	Gherkin	1	1
	Canned pineapple chunk	1	1

1. Thread the wooden skewer with 1 wiener piece, the pickle, another wiener piece, the pineapple chunk and the last wiener piece. Lay on the plate. Microwave, uncovered, on high (100%) for about 30 seconds until hot. Makes 1 kabob.

Frankfurter Flower

GET READY ✔
sharp knife, cutting board, small microwave-safe plate, wooden toothpicks

1.	Wieners	2	2

2. **Ketchup, for dipping**
   Prepared mustard, for dipping

1. Cut 1 wiener in half crosswise with the knife on the cutting board. Place the halves side by side on the small plate. Run the 2 wooden toothpicks through them so they will stay flat. Cut the second wiener into ½ inch (12 mm) pieces. Pierce each small piece of wiener with the wooden toothpick. Place the other end of the toothpick in the wiener base. Set on the plate. Microwave, uncovered, on high (100%) for 50 to 60 seconds until hot.

2. Dip into the ketchup and mustard. When the small pieces are eaten, cut up the 2 larger bottom wieners and pierce with the toothpicks. Makes 1.

Top Centre: Frankfurter Flower, above; Bottom: Pita Bean Snack, page 109; Right: Kid Kabobs, above

Sneaky Snack

GET READY ✓

sharp knife, cutting board, shallow microwave-safe bowl, measuring spoons, mixing spoon, oven mitts, hot pad

1.	**Wieners**	2	2
2.	**Grape (or apple or red currant) jelly**	1 tbsp.	15 mL
	Chili sauce (or ketchup)	1 tbsp.	15 mL

1. Cut each wiener into 6 or 7 pieces with the knife on the cutting board. Place all the pieces in the bowl.

2. Spoon the jelly and chili sauce over the wiener slices. Stir to coat. Microwave on high (100%) for 2 minutes. Stir. Use the oven mitts to remove the bowl to the hot pad. Serves 2.

You can't get any easier than this. Have paper napkins and wooden toothpicks handy.

Pita Bean Snack

GET READY ✓

1 quart (1 L) casserole dish, mixing spoon, sharp knife, cutting board, table spoon

1.	**Can of pork and beans**	14 oz.	398 mL
	Wieners, thinly sliced	2	2
2.	**Small pita breads**	4	4

1. Combine the pork and beans and wieners in the casserole dish. Stir. Cover. Microwave on high (100%) for about 2½ minutes until hot.

2. Cut open the tops of the pitas with the knife on the cutting board. Spoon about ¼ cup (60 mL) meat mixture into each. Makes 4.

Pictured on page 108.

French Fries

GET READY ✔
baking sheet, table fork, oven mitts, wire rack

1. Medium potatoes, peeled and cut into   6   6
   sticks or slices
   Salt, sprinkle
   Pepper, sprinkle

1. Place the oven rack in the centre position. Turn the oven on to 425°F (220°C). Grease the baking sheet. Spread the potato pieces in a single layer on the baking sheet. Bake in the oven for about 5 minutes until the centres are fairly tender when pierced with the fork. Use the oven mitts to remove the baking sheet to the wire rack. Sprinkle with the salt and pepper. Serves 6.

Kids of all ages will dive into these. These can be frozen in a single layer for 1 hour then transferred to a plastic freezer bag. To prepare, spread on a greased baking sheet and bake in a 425°F (220°C) oven for about 5 minutes.

Make this sandwich when you want to try a really different tasting grilled cheese sandwich.

Pineapple Grilled Cheese

GET READY ✓

frying pan, measuring spoons, small cup, mixing spoon, table knife, pancake lifter, medium plate

1. Canned crushed pineapple, well drained   2 tbsp.   30 mL
   Finely chopped pecans (optional)   2 tsp.   10 mL

2. Process cheese slices   2   2
   White (or whole-wheat) bread slices,   2   2
       buttered on 1 side

1. Heat the frying pan on medium-low. Combine the pineapple and pecans in the cup. Stir.

2. Put 1 cheese slice on the unbuttered side of a slice of bread. Use the knife to spread the pineapple mixture on top of the cheese. Lay the second cheese slice over the pineapple. Lay the second bread slice, butter-side up, on top of the cheese. Place the sandwich in the frying pan. When the bottom side is browned, use the pancake lifter to flip the sandwich over to brown the other side. Use the lifter to remove the sandwich to the plate. Makes 1 sandwich.

Snuggly Dogs

GET READY ✔

baking sheet, dry measures, measuring spoons, medium bowl, mixing spoon, pastry blender, liquid measures, table fork, rolling pin, sharp knife, cutting board, oven mitts, wire rack

1.	All-purpose flour	2 cups	500 mL
	Baking powder	4 tsp.	20 mL
	Granulated sugar	2 tbsp.	30 mL
	Salt	1 tsp.	5 mL
	Hard margarine	⅓ cup	75 mL
2.	Milk	¾ cup	175 mL
3.	Wieners, heated and wiped dry	12	12

1. Place the oven rack in the centre position. Turn the oven on to 425°F (220°C). Grease the baking sheet. Mix the first 4 ingredients in the bowl. Use the pastry blender to cut in the margarine until crumbly.

2. Add the milk. Stir with the fork until the dough forms a ball. Add a bit more milk, if necessary, to make a soft dough. Turn out onto a lightly floured surface. Knead 10 times. Roll the dough ¼ inch (6 mm) thick with the rolling pin. Cut into 12 rectangles with the knife on the cutting board.

3. Completely enclose each wiener in 1 portion of the dough. Dampen the edges of the dough. Press together to seal. Arrange on the baking sheet. Bake in the oven for 8 to 10 minutes until risen and golden brown. Use the oven mitts to remove the baking sheet to the wire rack. Makes 12 dogs.

Fun biscuits to fill hungry tummies.

Chewy Peanut Bars

GET READY ✔
9 × 13 inch (22 × 33 cm) oblong baking pan, dry measures, large saucepan, long-handled mixing spoon, hot pad

1.	Creamed honey	¾ cup	175 mL
	Smooth peanut butter	1 cup	250 mL
2.	Semisweet chocolate chips	1 cup	250 mL
	Large white marshmallows	10	10
3.	Crisp rice cereal	3 cups	750 mL
	Salted peanuts, finely chopped	1 cup	250 mL

1. Grease the pan. Set aside. Combine the honey and peanut butter in the saucepan. Heat on low, stirring occasionally, until just boiling. Remove the saucepan to the hot pad.

2. Add the chocolate chips and marshmallows. Stir until melted.

3. Add the cereal and peanuts. Grease your hands slightly. Pack the peanut mixture into the pan, pressing firmly and evenly. Chill. Cuts into 18 bars.

These are just like a popular chocolate bar.

Top Left: Chocolate Crisps, page 115; Top Right: Puffed Wheat Squares, page 115; Bottom Right: Chocolate Confetti, below

Chocolate Confetti

GET READY ✔

9 x 9 inch (22 x 22 cm) square baking pan, dry measures, large saucepan, long-handled mixing spoon, hot pad

1.	Hard margarine	¼ cup	60 mL
	Smooth peanut butter	½ cup	125 mL
	Semisweet chocolate chips	1 cup	250 mL
2.	Miniature coloured marshmallows	8 oz.	225 g

1. Grease the pan. Set aside. Melt the margarine and peanut butter in the saucepan. Stir in the chocolate chips until melted. Remove the saucepan to the hot pad. Cool so that you can hold your hand on the bottom of the saucepan.

2. Add the marshmallows. Stir until well coated. Press firmly in the pan with your hand. Chill. Cuts into 36 squares.

Variation: To the above ingredients add ½ cup (125 mL) chopped walnuts and/or ½ cup (125 mL) medium coconut.

Puffed Wheat Squares

GET READY ✔

8 x 8 inch (20 x 20 cm) square baking pan, dry measures, liquid measures, measuring spoons, small saucepan, long-handled mixing spoon, hot pad, large bowl

1.	Hard margarine	¼ cup	60 mL
	Light or dark corn syrup	⅓ cup	75 mL
	Brown sugar, packed	½ cup	125 mL
	Cocoa powder	1½ tbsp.	25 mL
2.	Puffed wheat cereal	6 cups	1.5 L

1. Grease the pan. Set aside. Combine the margarine, corn syrup, brown sugar and cocoa powder in the saucepan. Heat on medium, stirring constantly, until the mixture begins to bubble. Boil for 1½ minutes. Remove the saucepan to the hot pad.

2. Pour the mixture over the cereal in the bowl. Stir until all of the cereal is coated. Press firmly in the pan with your hand. Chill for 15 minutes before cutting. Cuts into 25 squares.

Pictured on page 114.

Chocolate Crisps

GET READY ✔

9 x 9 inch (22 x 22 cm) square baking pan, liquid measures, dry measures, large saucepan, long-handled mixing spoon, hot pad

1.	Liquid honey	¾ cup	175 mL
	Smooth peanut butter	1 cup	250 mL
2.	Semisweet chocolate chips	1 cup	250 mL
3.	Salted peanuts	1 cup	250 mL
	Crisp rice cereal	3 cups	750 mL

1. Grease the pan. Set aside. Melt the honey and peanut butter in the saucepan on low, stirring occasionally. Bring the mixture to a boil. Remove the saucepan to the hot pad.

2. Add the chocolate chips. Stir until melted.

3. Add the peanuts and cereal. Stir to coat. Press firmly in the pan with your hand. Chill well before cutting. Cuts into 36 squares.

Pictured on page 114.

Puffed Wheat Cake

GET READY ✔

large bowl, 9 × 9 inch (22 × 22 cm) square baking pan, dry measures, measuring spoons, large heavy saucepan, long-handled mixing spoon, candy thermometer, table spoon, hot pad

1.	Brown sugar, packed	1 cup	250 mL
	Creamed honey	½ cup	125 mL
	Hard margarine	½ cup	125 mL
	Cocoa powder	2 tbsp.	30 mL
2.	Vanilla flavouring	½ tsp.	2 mL
3.	Puffed wheat cereal	6 cups	1.5 L
	Crisp rice cereal	2 cups	500 mL

1. Grease the bowl and pan. Set aside. Combine the first 4 ingredients in the saucepan. Heat on medium-high, stirring often, until the mixture boils. Boil for 5 to 8 minutes until the temperature reaches the soft ball stage (about 235°F, 113°C, on the candy thermometer) or until a small spoonful forms a soft ball in cold water.

2. Remove the saucepan from the heat to the hot pad. Stir in the vanilla flavouring.

3. Combine both of the cereals in the bowl. Pour the hot honey mixture over the cereals. Stir to coat well. Press firmly in the pan with your hand. Let stand until cool and set. Cuts into 36 pieces.

Top: Puffed Wheat Cake, above
Bottom: Brownie Cupcakes, page 117

Brownie Cupcakes

GET READY ✔

dry measures, medium saucepan, long-handled mixing spoon, hot pad, measuring spoons, muffin pan (enough for 12 muffins), wooden toothpick, oven mitts, wire rack, small bowl, mixing spoon

1.	Semisweet chocolate baking squares (1 oz., 28 g, each), chopped	2	2
	Hard margarine	½ cup	125 mL
2.	Brown sugar, packed	1½ cups	375 mL
	All-purpose flour	1 cup	250 mL
	Large eggs, fork-beaten	2	2
	Vanilla flavouring	1 tsp.	5 mL
	Chopped pecans (or walnuts)	½ cup	125 mL
	Salt	¼ tsp.	1 mL
3.	CHOCOLATE ICING		
	Hard margarine, softened	3 tbsp.	50 mL
	Icing (confectioner's) sugar	1½ cups	375 mL
	Cocoa powder	⅓ cup	75 mL
	Water (or milk or coffee)	2 tbsp.	30 mL

1. Place the oven rack in the centre position. Turn the oven on to 350°F (175°C). Melt the chocolate and margarine in the saucepan on low, stirring often. Remove the saucepan to the hot pad.

2. Add the next 6 ingredients. Stir just enough to moisten. Grease the muffin pan. Spoon into the muffin pan, filling cups ½ full. Bake in the oven for 20 to 25 minutes until the wooden toothpick inserted in the centre comes out clean. Use the oven mitts to remove the muffin pan to the wire rack. Cool.

3. **Chocolate Icing:** Mix the margarine, icing sugar and cocoa powder in the small bowl. Add just enough of the water to make a barely pourable consistency. Spread on cooled cupcakes. Makes 12.

Pictured on page 116.

Jellied Marshmallows

GET READY ✓

8 × 8 inch (20 × 20 cm) square baking pan, waxed paper, liquid measures, small saucepan, long-handled mixing spoon, dry measures, measuring spoons, medium bowl, rubber spatula, electric mixer, small sieve, damp tea towel, sharp knife

1.			
Package of any flavour gelatin (jelly powder)		3 oz.	85 g
Boiling water		⅔ cup	150 mL
Granulated sugar		1 cup	250 mL
White corn syrup		3 tbsp.	50 mL

2. Icing (confectioner's) sugar, for coating

Top: Midnight Mints, page 119
Bottom: Jellied Marshmallows, above

1. Line the pan with the waxed paper. Combine the jelly powder and boiling water in the saucepan. Heat on low, stirring constantly, until dissolved. Add the granulated sugar, stirring constantly, until dissolved. Stir in the corn syrup. Turn into the bowl. Cool. Place the rubber spatula in the bowl. Chill for 10 minutes. Stir, scraping down sides of the bowl. Chill for 10 minute intervals, stirring and scraping sides down, until the mixture is almost as stiff as liquid honey, but not chunky. Beat on high with the mixer for 5 minutes until stiff. Pour into the waxed paper-lined pan. Chill overnight.

2. Use the sieve to sift some of the icing sugar onto the countertop or breadboard at least the size of the pan. Turn out the entire jellied square onto the icing sugar. Gently rub the damp tea towel over the waxed paper. Let stand for a few minutes. Pull off the waxed paper. Dust the top of the square with the icing sugar. Cut into squares with the knife, dusting each new cut surface with the icing sugar. Cuts into 25 squares.

good ✓

Midnight Mints

GET READY ✓

dry measures, large saucepan, long-handled mixing spoon, measuring spoons, liquid measures, hot pad, 9 × 9 inch (22 × 22 cm) square baking pan, small bowl, table knife, small saucepan

1.	**BOTTOM LAYER**		
	Hard margarine	½ cup	125 mL
	Granulated sugar	¼ cup	60 mL
	Cocoa powder	⅓ cup	75 mL
	Large egg, fork-beaten	1	1
2.	Graham cracker crumbs	1¾ cups	425 mL
	Finely chopped walnuts	½ cup	125 mL
	Fine coconut	¾ cup	175 mL
3.	**SECOND LAYER**		
	Hard margarine, softened	⅓ cup	75 mL
	Milk	3 tbsp.	50 mL
	Peppermint flavouring	1 tsp.	5 mL
	Icing (confectioner's) sugar	2 cups	500 mL
	Drops of green food colouring	2-3	2-3
4.	**TOP LAYER**		
	Semisweet chocolate chips	⅔ cup	150 mL
	Hard margarine	2 tbsp.	30 mL

(handwritten annotations: ¼c. ¼c beside Hard margarine, 1½tbsp beside Milk, 1½c beside Icing sugar, ⅔c + ¼c beside Semisweet chocolate chips, 4 tbsp. beside Hard margarine)

1. **Bottom Layer:** Combine the margarine, sugar and cocoa powder in the large saucepan on medium. Stir. Heat until the mixture boils. Remove 3 tbsp. (50 mL) mixture to the liquid measure. Add the egg slowly, stirring constantly. Add the egg mixture to the saucepan slowly, stirring constantly, until thickened. Remove the saucepan to the hot pad.

2. Stir in the graham crumbs, walnuts and coconut. Mix well. Grease the pan. Pack the crumb mixture very firmly in the pan.

3. **Second Layer:** Combine the margarine, milk, peppermint flavouring and icing sugar in the bowl. Beat together well. Add a bit more of the milk if needed to make the mixture spreadable. Tint green with the food colouring. Spread over the first layer with the knife.

4. **Top Layer:** Melt the chocolate chips and margarine in the small saucepan on low, stirring often. Cool. When cool but still runny, spread over the second layer. Chill. Cuts into 36 squares.

Pictured on page 118.

Chocolate Graham Squares

GET READY ✔

9 x 9 inch (22 x 22 cm) square baking pan, sharp knife, dry measures, liquid measures, large saucepan, long-handled mixing spoon, hot pad, measuring spoons, small bowl, electric mixer, rubber spatula

1.	Whole graham crackers	14	14
2.	Hard margarine	¾ cup	175 mL
	Brown sugar, packed	⅔ cup	150 mL
	Milk	½ cup	125 mL
3.	Semisweet chocolate chips	⅓ cup	75 mL
	Graham cracker crumbs	1¼ cups	300 mL
	Chopped walnuts	1 cup	250 mL
4.	Whole graham crackers	14	14
5.	**ICING**		
	Icing (confectioner's) sugar	1¼ cups	300 mL
	Hard margarine, softened	3 tbsp.	50 mL
	Cocoa powder	¼ cup	60 mL
	Hot prepared coffee	1½ tbsp.	25 mL

1. Line the ungreased pan with the first amount of graham crackers, trimming to fit with the knife.

2. Combine the margarine, brown sugar and milk in the saucepan. Stir. Heat on medium until the mixture comes to a boil.

3. Remove the saucepan to the hot pad. Add the chocolate chips. Stir to melt. Add the graham crumbs and walnuts. Mix. Pour over the crackers in the pan.

4. Cover with the second amount of whole graham crackers, trimming to fit. Cool.

5. **Icing:** Beat the icing sugar, margarine, cocoa powder and coffee in the bowl with the mixer, adding more liquid or icing sugar as needed for spreading consistency. Spread over the squares with the rubber spatula. Cover. Let stand for a few hours to soften the crackers before cutting. Cuts into 36 squares.

Pictured on page 121.

Crispy Rice Squares

GET READY ✔
8 × 8 inch (20 × 20 cm) square baking pan, dry measures, large saucepan, long-handled mixing spoon

1.	Hard margarine	¼ cup	60 mL
2.	Large white marshmallows	32	32
3.	Crisp rice cereal	5 cups	1.25 L

1. Grease the pan. Set aside. Melt the margarine in the saucepan.

2. Add the marshmallows. Stir on low until melted.

3. Add the cereal. Stir to coat well. Press firmly in the pan with your hand. Let stand for a few hours to set before cutting. Cuts into 25 squares.

Variation: Melt 3 tbsp. (50 mL) hard margarine and 1 cup (250 mL) semisweet chocolate chips on low, stirring often. Spread over the top.

Left: Crispy Rice Squares, above
Right: Chocolate Graham
Squares, page 120

Creamy Jelly Jiggles

GET READY ✔

9 × 13 inch (22 × 33 cm) oblong baking pan, medium bowl, mixing spoon, liquid measures, sharp knife (or cookie cutters)

1.	Envelopes of unflavoured gelatin (or 2 tbsp, 30 mL)	2	2
	Packages of lime-flavoured gelatin (jelly powder), 3 oz. (85 g) each	2	2
2.	Boiling water	1⅔ cups	400 mL
3.	Half-and-half (light cream)	⅔ cup	150 mL

1. Lightly grease the pan. Set aside. Pour both the unflavoured and flavoured gelatins into the bowl. Mix well.

2. Add the boiling water to the gelatin in the bowl. Stir until the gelatin dissolves.

3. Add the half-and-half. Stir. Pour into the pan. Chill for at least 3 hours. Cut into squares with the knife or into your favorite shapes with the cookie cutters.

These jiggles settle into layers for a different look. Do not freeze.

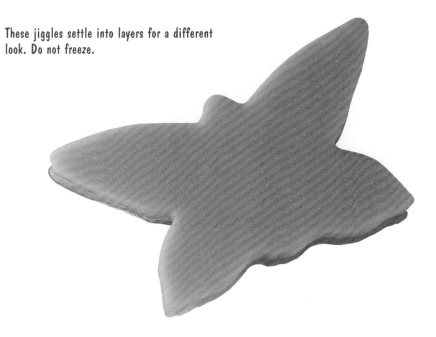

Jelly Jiggles

GET READY ✔

9 × 13 inch (22 × 33 cm) oblong baking pan, medium bowl, mixing spoon, liquid measures, sharp knife (or cookie cutters)

1.	Envelopes of unflavoured gelatin (or 2 tbsp, 30 mL)	2	2
	Envelopes of orange-flavoured gelatin (jelly powder), 3 oz. (85 g) each	2	2
2.	Boiling water	2½ cups	625 mL

1. Lightly grease the pan. Set aside. Pour both the unflavoured and flavoured gelatins into the bowl. Mix well.

2. Add the boiling water to the bowl. Stir until the gelatins are dissolved. Pour into the pan. Chill for at least 3 hours until set. Cut into squares with the knife or into your favorite shapes with the cookie cutters.

Great to have ready in the refrigerator! Do not freeze.

One is not enough!

Juice Jigglies

GET READY ✔
9 x 9 inch (22 x 22 cm) square baking pan, liquid measures, medium saucepan, long-handled mixing spoon, hot pad, sharp knife (or cookie cutters)

1.	Cold water	1½ cups	375 mL
	Envelopes of unflavoured gelatin (or 1/4 cup, 60 mL)	4	4
2.	Frozen concentrated grape juice (or cranberry or raspberry cocktail), see Note	12 oz.	341 mL

1. Grease the pan. Set aside. Put the water into the saucepan. Sprinkle the gelatin over the top. Let stand for 1 minute. Heat on medium, stirring frequently, until the mixture comes to a boil. Remove the saucepan to the hot pad.

2. Add the juice concentrate. Stir until dissolved. Pour the mixture into the pan. Chill for 1 to 2 hours until set. Cut into squares with the knife or into your favorite shapes with the cookie cutters.

Note: Do not use a citrus concentrate such as orange, lemon or pineapple.

Apple Lime Freezies

GET READY ✔

liquid measures, medium saucepan, hot pad, long-handled mixing spoon, dry measures, 10 plastic drink cups (5 oz., 142 mL, size), foil, 10 wooden freezer pop sticks (available at craft stores)

1.	Apple juice	2 cups	500 mL
2.	Package of lime-flavoured gelatin (jelly powder)	3 oz.	85 g
3.	Apple juice	2 cups	500 mL
	Applesauce	1 cup	250 mL

1. Pour the first amount of apple juice into the saucepan. Heat on medium-high until just starting to boil.

2. Remove the saucepan to the hot pad. Add the lime gelatin. Stir until dissolved.

3. Add the second amount of apple juice and applesauce. Stir. Pour the mixture into the drink cups to ¾ full. Place a piece of foil over each cup. Cut a small slit in the middle. Fit the freezer pop sticks in through the foil. Freeze. To remove the freezie, run hot water on the bottom of the cup until the freezie slides out. Makes 10 freezies.

The colour is great! And the lime taste is refreshing.

A chewy cookie. Store the cookies in a covered container with waxed paper between the layers.

Chocolate Oat Chippers

GET READY ✔

dry measures, measuring spoons, large bowl, electric mixer, mixing spoon, cookie sheet, oven mitts, wire rack, pancake lifter, waxed paper

1.			
Hard margarine, softened	½ cup	125 mL	
Brown sugar, packed	1 cup	250 mL	
Large egg	1	1	
Vanilla flavouring	½ tsp.	2 mL	
2.			
All-purpose flour	1 cup	250 mL	
Quick rolled oats (not instant)	1 cup	250 mL	
Baking soda	½ tsp.	2 mL	
Salt	¼ tsp.	1 mL	
Semisweet chocolate chips	1 cup	250 mL	
Chopped walnuts (optional)	½ cup	125 mL	

1. Place the oven rack in the centre position. Turn the oven on to 350°F (175°C). Put the margarine, brown sugar, egg and vanilla flavouring into the bowl. Beat with the mixer on medium speed until smooth.

2. Add the remaining 6 ingredients. Stir with the spoon until all of the flour is mixed in. Grease the cookie sheet. Drop by rounded tablespoonfuls, 2 inches (5 cm) apart, onto the cookie sheet. This will allow room for the cookies to spread out. Bake in the oven for 10 to 12 minutes. Use the oven mitts to remove the cookie sheet to the wire rack. Let stand for 2 minutes. Use the pancake lifter to remove the cookies to the waxed paper on the counter. Cool completely. Makes about 3 dozen cookies.

Chocolate Bar Cookies

GET READY ✔

dry measures, medium bowl, mixing spoon, measuring spoons, rubber spatula, thick plastic bag, rolling pin, cookie sheet, oven mitts, wire rack, pancake lifter, waxed paper

1.	Hard margarine, softened	½ cup	125 mL
	Brown sugar, packed	⅓ cup	75 mL
	Granulated sugar	⅓ cup	75 mL
2.	Vanilla flavouring	1 tsp.	5 mL
	Large egg, fork-beaten	1	1
3.	All-purpose flour	1¼ cups	300 mL
	Baking soda	½ tsp.	2 mL
	Salt	¼ tsp.	1 mL
4.	Butter crunch chocolate bars (1½ oz., 39 g, each)	2	2

1. Place the oven rack in the centre position. Turn the oven on to 375°F (190°C). Cream the margarine and both sugars together in the bowl until smooth.

2. Stir in the vanilla flavouring and egg.

3. Add the flour, baking soda and salt. Mix well, scraping down the sides of the bowl with the spatula.

4. Place the chocolate bars in the plastic bag. Break the bars into chunky pieces by hitting them with the rolling pin. Stir the chunks into the dough. Drop by rounded tablespoonfuls, about 2 inches (5 cm) apart, onto the ungreased cookie sheet. Bake in the oven for 10 minutes until the edges are browned. Centres will stay soft. Use the oven mitts to remove the cookie sheet to the wire rack. Let stand for 1 minute. Use the pancake lifter to remove the cookies to the waxed paper to cool completely. Makes 24 cookies.

Dotted with chocolate. Soft and chewy. Just right with a glass of milk.

Let an adult show you how to core the apple the first time you make this. For a chewy texture, use Crumble Topping, page 85, to fill the cavity instead of the brown sugar and cinnamon.

Microwave Baked Apple

GET READY ✔

vegetable peeler, small microwave-safe bowl, measuring spoons, small cup, small table spoon

1.	Medium cooking apple (such as McIntosh)	1	1
2.	Brown sugar, packed	1 tbsp.	15 mL
	Ground cinnamon	⅛ tsp.	0.5 mL
3.	Margarine	1 tsp.	5 mL

1. Wash the apple well. Remove the stem. Pierce down into the middle of the apple several times with the vegetable peeler, digging out as much of the core as possible. Put the apple into the bowl.

2. Combine the brown sugar and cinnamon in the cup. Stir. Sprinkle into the middle of the apple.

3. Top the apple with the margarine. Microwave on high (100%) for 2 minutes until the apple is tender. Cool slightly. Makes 1 apple.

Baked Apples

GET READY ✓
vegetable peeler, 1 quart (1 L) casserole dish, measuring spoons, small cup, small table spoon

1.	Medium cooking apples (such as McIntosh)	2	2
2.	Raisins (or currants)	1 tbsp.	15 mL
3.	Brown sugar, packed	2 tbsp.	30 mL
	Ground cinnamon	⅟₁₆ tsp.	0.5 mL
4.	Margarine	1 tsp.	5 mL
	Water	3 tbsp.	50 mL

1. Wash the apples well. Remove the stems. Pierce down into the apples several times with the vegetable peeler, digging out as much of the core as possible. Peel a narrow strip around the top of the apples. Place in the casserole dish.

2. Divide the raisins in half. Fill the apple cavities with the raisins.

3. Stir the brown sugar and cinnamon together in the cup. Press on top of the raisins. Sprinkle the remaining mixture over the apples.

4. Top each cavity with the margarine. Pour the water into the dish. Cover. Microwave on high (100%) for about 2 minutes. Microwave on medium (50%) for about 3 minutes until apples are fork tender, rotating dish ½ turn two times if you don't have a turntable. Let stand, covered, for 3 minutes. Spoon the juice over apples. Serves 2.

Made in the microwave, this is a great
after-school snack for you and a friend.

Turtle Chocolates

GET READY ✔

2 heavy medium saucepans, measuring spoons, 2 long-handled mixing spoons, cookie sheet, waxed paper, dry measures, hot pad, table fork

1.	Caramels	48	48
	Milk	3 tbsp.	50 mL
2.	Chopped pecans	2 cups	500 mL
3.	**COATING**		
	Semisweet chocolate chips	2 cups	500 mL

1. Unwrap the caramels and put them into one of the saucepans. Add the milk. Heat on low, stirring often, until the caramels are melted.

2. Cover the cookie sheet with the waxed paper. Grease the paper well. Add the pecans to the melted caramels. Stir. Leave on very low heat to keep from getting hard. Drop by rounded teaspoonfuls onto the waxed paper. Chill for 1 hour until firm.

3. **Coating:** Place the chocolate chips in the second saucepan. Heat on low, stirring often, until melted and smooth. Remove the saucepan to the hot pad. Drop 1 clump of caramel mixture at a time into the chocolate. Slide the fork under the piece and lift up to let the excess chocolate drip back into the saucepan. Repeat with the remaining pieces. Place back on the waxed paper. Chill. Makes 3 to 3½ dozen chocolates.

    Pictured on page 3 and below.

Left: Turtle Chocolates, above
Right: Marshmallow Delights, page 131

Marshmallow Delights

GET READY ✔

table knife, double boiler, dry measures, liquid measures, long-handled mixing spoon, hot pad, medium bowl, table fork, waxed paper

1.	Butterscotch toffee bars (2 oz., 56 g, each), or 23 unwrapped bite-sized toffees (such as Mackintosh's)	3	3
	Hard margarine	¼ cup	60 mL
	Sweetened condensed milk	⅔ cup	150 mL
2.	Crisp rice cereal	4 cups	1 L
	Large white marshmallows	30-35	30-35

1. Break up the toffee bars by placing one bar in the palm of your hand. Hit the bar with the handle of the knife. Put the pieces into the top of the double boiler. Add the margarine and condensed milk. Put some hot water in the bottom of the double boiler. Set the top part in. Heat on medium-high, stirring occasionally, until melted and smooth. Remove the double boiler to the hot pad. Keep the toffee mixture over the hot water.

2. Measure the cereal into the bowl. Stick the fork into the end of one of the marshmallows. Roll the marshmallow in the toffee mixture to coat the bottom and sides. Hold the marshmallow over the toffee mixture to drain. Roll in the cereal, using your other hand to coat the bottom and sides. Push the marshmallow off of the fork. Place the uncoated end down onto the waxed paper. Repeat with the rest of the marshmallows. If the toffee mixture gets stiff, heat the water underneath until it begins to boil again. Makes 30 to 35 marshmallow treats.

Pictured on pages 3 and 130.

Fiddle Diddles

GET READY ✔

dry measures, liquid measures, small saucepan, long-handled mixing spoon, hot pad, measuring spoons, small table spoon, large sheet of waxed paper, covered container

1.	Hard margarine	½ cup	125 mL
	Granulated sugar	2 cups	500 mL
	Milk	½ cup	125 mL
2.	Cocoa powder	6 tbsp.	100 mL
	Quick-cooking rolled oats (not instant)	3 cups	750 mL
	Medium coconut	½ cup	125 mL
	Chopped walnuts	½ cup	125 mL
	Salt, just a pinch		
	Vanilla flavouring	1 tsp.	5 mL

1. Put the margarine, sugar and milk into the saucepan. Heat on medium, stirring often, until the mixture comes to a boil. Remove the saucepan to the hot pad.

2. Add the remaining 6 ingredients. Stir well. Drop by rounded small table spoonfuls onto the waxed paper. Cool completely. Store, covered, in the container with waxed paper between the layers. Makes about 40 cookies.

Pictured below and on page 133.

A no-bake cookie that always turns out. Chocolate-flavoured and nutty.

Fruity S'Mores

GET READY ✔

long-handled barbecue fork, small plate

1.	Large white marshmallow	1	1
2.	Whole graham crackers	2	2
	Squares of thin milk chocolate bar	2-6	2-6
	Thin slices of strawberry (or	2	2
	halves of seedless grapes)		

1. Stick the fork in the end of the marshmallow, about ½ way through. Hold it over a fire or very hot burner until it is toasty brown and soft.

2. Place one of the graham cracker squares on the plate. Place the chocolate on the square. Push the marshmallow on top of the chocolate. Place the fruit slices on top of the marshmallow. Top with the second graham cracker. Push down, holding a few moments so the chocolate begins to melt. Makes 1 treat.

Left: Fruity S'Mores, above; Right: Fiddle Diddles, page 132

Fast. Easy. Looks fabulous! Tastes fabulous!

All Around S'Mores

GET READY ✔

table knife, small microwave-safe plate

1.	Round graham crackers	4	4
	Hazelnut chocolate spread		
	Large white or coloured marshmallows	2	2

1. Use the knife to spread all 4 crackers with the chocolate spread. Place 2 of the crackers on the plate. Place the marshmallows on the top. Microwave on high (100%) for 15 seconds. Remove the plate from the microwave. Place the other 2 crackers on top of each marshmallow. Push down slightly until the marshmallows spread to the outer edges of the crackers. Makes 2 S'Mores.

    Pictured on page 73 and above.

Variation 1: Use digestive biscuits or sugar cookies in place of the graham crackers.

Variation 2: Sprinkle chocolate chips or butterscotch chips on the bottom of 2 of the crackers. Microwave on high (100%) for 1 minute. Place the marshmallows on top. Microwave on high (100%) for 10 seconds. Top with the remaining crackers.

Choco-Peanut Butter Dreams

GET READY ✔

liquid measures, medium bowl, electric mixer, dry measures, baking sheet, small table spoon, covered container

1.	Envelope of dessert topping (not prepared)	1	1
	Milk	½ cup	125 mL
2.	Smooth peanut butter	½ cup	125 mL
3.	Milk	1 cup	250 mL
	Instant chocolate pudding powder (4 serving size)	1	1
4.	Package of chocolate wafers (about 48)	7 oz.	200 g

1. Combine the dessert topping and first amount of milk in the bowl. Beat with the mixer on high speed until thickened.

2. Add the peanut butter. Beat on low speed until mixed.

3. Add the second amount of milk and pudding powder. Beat on low speed until blended. Beat on high speed for 2 minutes.

4. Place 24 of the wafers on the ungreased baking sheet. Put a heaping spoonful of the mixture on each wafer. Top with the remaining 24 wafers. Freeze, uncovered, for 3 hours. Put into the covered container to store. Makes 24 "dreams."

That wonderful combination of chocolate and peanut butter. A great treat to have in the freezer.

Have your friends help you make these—and then enjoy!

Coated Marshmallows

GET READY ✔

measuring spoons, small saucepan, liquid measures, dry measures, long-handled mixing spoon, hot pad, large bowl, table fork, waxed paper

1.	Hard margarine	1 tbsp.	15 mL
	Golden corn syrup	⅔ cup	150 mL
	Brown sugar, packed	⅓ cup	75 mL
2.	Smooth peanut butter	½ cup	125 mL
	Vanilla flavouring	½ tsp.	2 mL
3.	Crisp rice cereal	5 cups	1.25 L
4.	Large white or coloured marshmallows	24	24

1. Melt the margarine in the saucepan over medium. Add the corn syrup and brown sugar. Heat, stirring constantly, until boiling. Remove the saucepan to the hot pad.

2. Add the peanut butter. Stir until melted. Add the vanilla. Stir.

3. Put the cereal into the bowl.

4. Use the fork to dip each marshmallow into the peanut butter mixture until completely coated. Roll in the cereal. Set on the waxed paper to cool. Makes 24 marshmallows.

Weekend Treats

Mock Champagne

GET READY ✔

liquid measures, 2 quart (2 L) pitcher, long-handled mixing spoon, drinking glasses, sharp knife, cutting board

1.	White grape juice, chilled	4 cups	1 L
	Club soda, chilled	4 cups	1 L
2.	Ice cubes, per glass	2-3	2-3
	Lime (or lemon) slices, for garnish	10	10

1. Pour the white grape juice into the pitcher. Chill for about 2 hours. Immediately before serving, pour the club soda into the grape juice. Stir gently.

2. Place some ice cubes in each glass. Fill with the drink mixture. Make a cut half way through the lime slice using the sharp knife on the cutting board. Fit over the edge of each glass. Makes about 7½ cups (1.9 L).

A fine-tasting bubbly drink, almost like the real thing! Do not freeze.

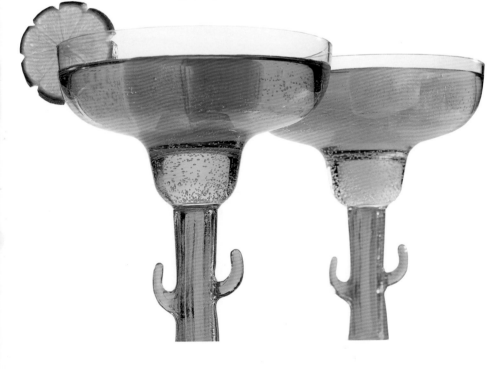

A smooth fruit punch. Do not freeze.

Party Punch

GET READY ✔
2 quart (2 L) pitcher (or small punch bowl), liquid measures, long-handled mixing spoon, drinking glasses (or punch cups)

1.	Frozen concentrated orange juice, thawed	½ x 12½ oz.	½ x 355 mL
	Frozen concentrated lemonade, thawed	½ x 12½ oz.	½ x 355 mL
	Pineapple juice	2 cups	500 mL
2.	Ginger ale	4 cups	1 L
3.	Ice cubes, per glass	2-3	2-3
	Maraschino cherries, for garnish	10	10
	Orange slices, for garnish	10	10

1. Empty the concentrated orange juice and lemonade into the pitcher or punch bowl. Add the pineapple juice. Stir well. Chill until ready to serve.

2. Add the ginger ale to the juice mixture. Stir gently. If using a punch bowl, empty the juices from the pitcher into the bowl. Add the ginger ale. Stir gently.

3. Put 2 or 3 ice cubes into each glass or punch cup. Fill with the punch. Makes 7½ cups (1.9 L).

Vanilla Milk Shake

GET READY ✔

ice-cream scoop, liquid measures, measuring spoons, blender, drinking glass, drinking straw

1.			
Rounded scoops of vanilla ice cream	2	2
Milk	¾ cup	175 mL
Instant vanilla pudding powder	1 tbsp.	15 mL
Vanilla flavouring	½ tsp.	2 mL

1. Place all 4 ingredients in the blender. Place the lid on the blender. Process the ice cream mixture for about 20 seconds until smooth and frothy. Serve in the glass with the straw. Makes about 2 cups (500 mL).

CHOCOLATE MILK SHAKE: Leave out the vanilla flavouring. Add 2 tbsp. (30 mL) chocolate syrup.

STRAWBERRY MILK SHAKE: Leave out the vanilla flavouring. Increase the milk to 1 cup (250 mL) and add ½ cup (125 mL) sliced strawberries. Strawberry ice cream can also be used instead of the vanilla ice cream.

ORANGE MILK SHAKE: Leave out the vanilla flavouring and milk. Add 1 cup (250 mL) orange soft drink.

CHOCO BANANA MILK SHAKE: Leave out the vanilla flavouring. Add 2 tbsp. (30 mL) chocolate syrup and 1 ripe banana, sliced.

PURPLE COW: Leave out the vanilla flavouring. Add ½ cup (125 mL) grape soft drink.

1. Strawberry Milk Shake
2. Orange Milk Shake
3. Choco Banana Milk Shake
4. Purple Cow
5. Vanilla Milk Shake
6. Chocolate Milk Shake

Hot Cocoa

GET READY ✔

measuring spoons, mug that holds 1 cup (250 mL), small mixing spoon, liquid measures, small saucepan

1.	**Cocoa powder**	1½ tsp.	7 mL
	Granulated sugar	1½ tsp.	7 mL
	Water	1½ tsp.	7 mL
2.	**Milk**	¾ cup	175 mL
3.	**Miniature marshmallows (or frozen whipped topping)**	3-4	3-4

1. Mix the cocoa powder, sugar and water in the mug until smooth.

2. Pour the milk into the saucepan. Heat on medium, stirring slowly to make sure it does not burn, until steaming. Carefully pour the milk into the mug. Stir.

3. Top with the marshmallows. Serves 1.

Easy to make for yourself but you can also make it for your friends.

Framed Eggs

GET READY ✔

frying pan with lid, measuring spoons, table knife, drinking glass, pancake lifter, large plate

1.	Margarine	2 tsp.	10 mL
	White (or whole-wheat) bread slice (1 inch, 2.5 cm, thick)	1	1
2.	Margarine	½ tsp.	2 mL
	Large egg	1	1
	Salt, sprinkle		
	Pepper, sprinkle		

1. Heat the frying pan on medium. Spread the first amount of margarine on both sides of the bread slice with the table knife. Place the drinking glass upside down on the centre of the bread slice. Press to cut out a round piece. Place both the bread slice and round piece of bread in the frying pan. Brown 1 side of each. Turn the heat to medium-low. Use the pancake lifter to turn both pieces over.

2. Melt the second amount of margarine in the hole in the bread slice. Break the egg into the hole. Sprinkle with the salt and pepper. Place the lid on the frying pan. Cook slowly until the white of the egg is set. Remove the lid. Remove the egg and toast with the lifter to the plate. Garnish with the toasted round piece. Serves 1.

A picturesque way to serve eggs.
Do not freeze.

Start the day right or even enjoy these for lunch or supper. For fun, try a creative design such as your initials.

Pancakes

GET READY ✔

small bowl, mixing spoon, liquid measures, measuring spoons, dry measures, no-stick cooking spray, large table spoon, frying pan, pancake lifter, large plate

1.	Large eggs	2	2
2.	Milk	1 cup	250 mL
	Cooking oil	2 tbsp.	30 mL
3.	All-purpose flour	1¼ cups	300 mL
	Granulated sugar	1 tbsp.	15 mL
	Baking powder	1 tbsp.	15 mL
	Salt	¼ tsp.	1 mL

1. Break the eggs into the bowl. Stir until the eggs are fairly smooth and a bit bubbly.

2. Add the milk and cooking oil. Mix.

3. Add the remaining 4 ingredients. Stir just until moistened. Heat the frying pan until a few drops of water bounce all over. Spray with the no-stick cooking spray. Scoop spoonfuls of the batter into the frying pan using the large table spoon. When the tops are bubbly and the edges are a bit dry, turn over with the pancake lifter to brown the other side. Remove with the lifter to the plate. Repeat until all the batter is used. Makes 18 round pancakes.

French Toast

GET READY ✔

9 inch (22 cm) pie plate, table fork, measuring spoons, frying pan, pancake lifter, large plate, table spoon, sieve

1.	Large egg	1	1
	Milk (or water)	3 tbsp.	50 mL
	Salt	⅛ tsp.	0.5 mL
	Vanilla flavouring	⅛ tsp.	0.5 mL
2.	Margarine	2 tsp.	10 mL
3.	French bread slices, cut 1 inch (2.5 cm) thick	2-3	2-3
4.	Icing (confectioner's) sugar, sprinkle		

1. Break the egg into the pie plate. Beat with the fork. Add the milk, salt and vanilla flavouring. Beat with the fork to mix.

2. Melt the margarine in the frying pan on medium.

3. Dip the bread slices, 1 at a time, into the egg mixture, turning to coat both sides. Place the slices in the frying pan. Brown 1 side. Use the pancake lifter to turn the slices over. Brown the other side. Use the lifter to remove the slices to the large plate.

4. Put a spoonful of the icing sugar into the sieve. Shake it gently over top of the slices to give a light sprinkle. Serves 2.

Serve with maple syrup.
A scrumptious breakfast.

Great! Lots of cheese.

Easy Oven Omelet

GET READY ✔

deep 9 inch (22 cm) pie plate (or 1 quart, 1 L, casserole dish), measuring spoons, medium bowl, electric mixer, dry measures, table knife, oven mitts, wire rack

1.			
	Large eggs	6	6
	Can of skim evaporated milk	13½ oz.	385 mL
	All-purpose flour	1 tbsp.	15 mL
	Salt	¼ tsp.	1 mL
2.	Grated Cheddar (or Swiss) cheese	1½ cups	375 mL
	Green onions, sliced	2	2
	Medium tomato, chopped	1	1

1. Place the oven rack in the centre position. Turn the oven on to 325°F (160°C). Grease the pie plate. Put the eggs, evaporated milk, flour and salt into the bowl. Beat on medium with the mixer.

2. Scatter the remaining 3 ingredients in the bottom of the pie plate. Pour the egg mixture carefully over top. Bake in the oven for 60 to 65 minutes until the knife inserted in the centre of the omelet comes out clean. Use the oven mitts to remove the pie plate to the wire rack. Serves 4.

Fruit Waffles À La Mode

GET READY ✔

baking sheet, table spoon, liquid measures, oven mitts, wire rack, pancake lifter, medium plates, ice-cream scoop

1.	Frozen plain (or buttermilk) waffles	2	2
2.	Canned cherry pie filling	½ cup	125 mL
3.	Small scoops of vanilla ice cream	2	2
	Maraschino cherries	2	2

1. Place the oven rack in the centre position. Turn the oven on to 350°F (175°C). Place both waffles on the ungreased baking sheet.

2. Spoon ¼ cup (60 mL) of the pie filling onto each waffle. Bake in the oven for 20 minutes until the pie filling is hot and bubbling and the waffle is crisp. Use the oven mitts to remove the baking sheet to the wire rack. Use the pancake lifter to place the waffles on the plates.

3. Top each hot waffle with 1 scoop of the ice cream. Top each scoop with a maraschino cherry. Makes 2 waffles.

Pictured on page 137, at right and on back cover.

As delicious as cherry pie. Use a variety of pie fillings for different tastes. Try peach or raisin. Gets top marks for presentation and eye appeal.

Crispy Fruit Pizza

GET READY ✔

dry measures, large saucepan, 3 mixing spoons, hot pad, 12 inch (30 cm) pizza pan, small bowl, electric mixer, rubber spatula, measuring spoons, small cup, pastry brush, liquid measures, medium bowl, table spoon

1.	**CRUST**		
	Hard margarine	¼ cup	60 mL
	Large marshmallows	32	32
2.	Crisp rice cereal	5 cups	1.25 L
3.	**TOPPING**		
	Cream cheese, softened	8 oz.	250 g
	Icing (confectioner's) sugar	2 cups	500 mL
	Cocoa powder	¼ cup	60 mL
4.	Small strawberries, halved	16	16
	Banana, sliced	1	1
	Kiwifruit, halved lengthwise and sliced	2	2
5.	**GLAZE**		
	Apricot jam	2 tbsp.	30 mL
	Water	1½ tsp.	7 mL
6.	Envelope of dessert topping (not prepared)	1	1
	Milk	⅔ cup	150 mL
	Vanilla flavouring	½ tsp.	2 mL

1. **Crust:** Combine the margarine and marshmallows in the saucepan. Heat on medium-low, stirring often, until melted.

2. Remove the saucepan to the hot pad. Add the cereal. Stir until the cereal is well coated. Grease the pizza pan. Press the cereal mixture evenly in the pan with your wet fingers. Cool.

3. **Topping:** Put the cream cheese, icing sugar and cocoa powder into the small bowl. Use the mixer to beat on low just until moistened. Beat on medium until smooth. Spread over the cooled pizza crust with the rubber spatula.

4. Arrange the strawberries, banana and kiwifruit over the chocolate topping in a fancy design.

5. **Glaze:** Mix the
   jam and water in
   the cup. Use the pastry
   brush to dab the fruit with the
   jam mixture. The glaze will prevent
   the fruit from turning brown.

6. Beat the dessert topping, milk and vanilla flavouring in the medium bowl until
   thickened. Dab on top of the pizza. Cuts into 8 to 10 wedges.

Dark Blue Heaven Dessert

GET READY ✔

9 × 13 inch (22 × 33 cm) oblong baking pan, small mixing spoon, rubber spatula, measuring spoons, small cup, dry measures, wooden toothpick, oven mitts, wire rack

1.	Can of crushed pineapple, with juice	19 oz.	540 mL
	Can of blueberry pie filling	19 oz.	540 mL
	Yellow cake mix (2 layer size)	1	1
2.	Granulated sugar	1 tbsp.	15 mL
	Ground cinnamon	½ tsp.	2 mL
3.	Hard margarine, thinly sliced	1 cup	250 mL
	Chopped walnuts	¾ cup	175 mL

1. Place the oven rack in the centre position. Turn the oven on to 350°F (175°C). Grease the pan. Spread the pineapple with juice in the pan. Drop small spoonfuls of the pie filling here and there over the pineapple. Use the spatula to empty the can. Sprinkle the dry cake mix evenly over the pie filling.

2. Mix the sugar and cinnamon in the small cup. Sprinkle evenly over the cake mix.

3. Arrange the margarine slices over the top of the cake mix. Sprinkle with the walnuts. Bake in the oven for 45 to 55 minutes. The wooden toothpick inserted in the centre of the cake should come out clean. Use the oven mitts to remove the pan to the wire rack. Cuts into 15 pieces.

This easy dessert looks as delicious as it tastes. Serve in squares, warm with ice cream, or cold with whipped cream or ice cream.

Raisin Cobbler

GET READY ✔

1½ quart (1.5 L) casserole dish, measuring spoons, 2 mixing spoons, medium bowl, liquid measures, dry measures, oven mitts, wire rack, wooden toothpick

1.	Can of raisin pie filling	19 oz.	540 mL
	Lemon juice	1 tsp.	5 mL
2.	Large egg	1	1
	Cooking oil	⅓ cup	75 mL
	Milk	⅓ cup	75 mL
3.	All-purpose flour	1½ cups	375 mL
	Granulated sugar	⅓ cup	75 mL
	Baking powder	2 tsp.	10 mL
	Salt	½ tsp.	2 mL

1. Place the oven rack in the centre position. Turn the oven on to 400°F (205°C). Pour the raisin pie filling into the ungreased casserole dish. Add the lemon juice. Stir into the filling. Place the casserole, uncovered, in the oven to heat while preparing the topping.

2. Break the egg into the bowl. Use the spoon to beat until fairly smooth. Add the cooking oil and milk to the egg. Stir.

3. Add the flour, sugar, baking powder and salt. Stir just until moistened. Use the oven mitts to remove the casserole dish to the wire rack. Drop the batter by rounded tablespoonfuls over top of the filling. Return the casserole dish to the oven. Bake, uncovered, in the oven for 20 to 25 minutes. The wooden toothpick inserted in the centre of the topping should come out clean. Use the oven mitts to remove the casserole dish to the wire rack. Serve warm. Serves 6.

If your favorite filling is blueberry or cherry, use it rather than the raisin. Good and easy.

Tomato Soup Cake

GET READY ✔

9 x 9 inch (22 x 22 cm) square baking pan, measuring spoons, dry measures, large bowl, electric mixer, rubber spatula, mixing spoon, wooden toothpick, oven mitts, wire rack

1.			
Hard margarine, softened	6 tbsp.	100 mL
Can of condensed tomato soup	10 oz.	284 mL
All-purpose flour	1½ cups	375 mL
Granulated sugar	1 cup	250 mL
Large egg	1	1
Baking soda	1 tsp.	5 mL
Ground cinnamon	1 tsp.	5 mL
Ground allspice	¼ tsp.	1 mL
Salt	¼ tsp.	1 mL
2. Raisins (optional)	¾ cup	175 mL
Cream Cheese Icing, page 153		

1. Place the oven rack in the centre position. Turn the oven on to 350°F (175°C). Grease the inside of the pan. Measure the first 9 ingredients into the bowl. Use the mixer to beat on low until the flour is just moistened. Beat on medium, scraping down the sides of the bowl 2 or 3 times with the rubber spatula, until the batter is smooth.

2. Add the raisins. Stir to distribute them. Turn the batter into the pan. Bake in the oven for about 35 minutes. The wooden toothpick inserted in the centre of the cake should come out clean. Use the oven mitts to remove the pan to the wire rack. Cool. Ice. Makes 1 cake.

Pictured on page 153.

Tomato Soup Cake, page 152, is an old-fashioned cake that is prepared in one bowl. The Cream Cheese Icing, below, makes this cake really yummy.

Cream Cheese Icing

GET READY ✔
measuring spoons, dry measures, medium bowl, electric mixer, table knife

1.			
Cream cheese, softened	4 oz.	125 g
Hard margarine, softened	2 tbsp.	30 mL
Icing (confectioner's) sugar	1½ cups	375 mL
Vanilla flavouring	½ tsp.	2 mL

1. Combine the cream cheese, margarine, icing sugar and vanilla flavouring in the bowl. Use the mixer to beat on low just until moistened. Beat on medium until smooth and fluffy. Spread over Tomato Soup Cake, page 152. Makes 1¼ cups (300 mL), enough to ice a 9 x 9 inch (22 x 22 cm) cake.

Grilled Cheese Sandwich

GET READY ✔

frying pan, measuring spoons, table knife, pancake lifter, small plate, sharp knife

1.	Margarine	2 tsp.	10 mL
	White (or whole-wheat) bread slices	2	2
	Process cheese slice	1	1

1. Heat the frying pan on medium-high. Spread the margarine on 1 side of both bread slices. Place 1 slice, buttered side down, in the frying pan. Place the cheese slice on top. Cover with the second bread slice, buttered side up. When the bottom side is browned, use the pancake lifter to turn the sandwich over. Brown the other side. Use the lifter to remove the sandwich to the plate. Cut in half. Makes 1 sandwich.

Pictured on page 155.

Meaty Buns

GET READY ✔

dry measures, measuring spoons, medium bowl, mixing spoon, table knife, baking sheet, oven mitts, wire rack, pancake lifter, plate

1.	Can of processed meat, mashed	12 oz.	340 g
	Grated Cheddar cheese	2 cups	500 mL
	Finely chopped green pepper	½ cup	125 mL
	Can of condensed tomato soup	10 oz.	284 mL
	Worcestershire sauce	2 tsp.	10 mL
	Sweet pickle relish	2 tbsp.	30 mL
	Onion salt	½ tsp.	2 mL
	Hamburger buns, split in half	8	8

1. Place the oven rack in the top position. Turn the oven on to broil. Combine the first 7 ingredients in the bowl. Mix well. Makes 4 cups (1 L) filling. Divide the mixture among the bun halves. Spread to the edges. Place on the ungreased baking sheet. Broil to melt the cheese. Use the oven mitts to remove the baking sheet to the wire rack. Use the pancake lifter to remove the buns to the plate. Makes 16 bun halves.

Pictured on page 155.

Scrambled Egg Sandwich

GET READY ✔

cutting board, measuring spoons, table knife, table fork, small bowl, frying pan, long-handled mixing spoon, sharp knife, cutting board, pancake lifter, small plate

1.	**White (or whole-wheat) bread slices**	**2**	**2**
	Margarine	**2 tsp.**	**10 mL**
2.	**Large egg**	**1**	**1**
	Water	**1 tbsp.**	**15 mL**
	Margarine	**½ tsp.**	**2 mL**
3.	**Salt, sprinkle (optional)**		
	Pepper, sprinkle (optional)		
	Ketchup	**2 tsp.**	**10 mL**

1. Place the bread slices on the cutting board. Spread the first amount of margarine on 1 side of both bread slices.

2. Mix the egg and water with the fork in the bowl. Melt the second amount of margarine in the frying pan on medium. Add the egg mixture. Stir constantly until cooked.

3. Spread the cooked egg mixture on the buttered side of 1 slice of bread. Sprinkle with the salt and pepper. Spread the ketchup on the buttered side of the second slice of bread. Place the second slice over the top of the egg mixture, unbuttered side up. Cut in half on the cutting board. Use the pancake lifter to transfer the sandwich to the plate. Makes 1 sandwich.

This Scrambled Egg Sandwich, pictured at top right, is quick to prepare for lunch or a snack. Do not freeze. Shown at top left, the Grilled Cheese Sandwich, page 154, goes great with a bowl of hot soup. Use your favorite canned meat to make Meaty Buns, page 154, shown at the bottom.

Fried Onion Dogs

GET READY ✔

measuring spoons, frying pan, long-handled mixing spoon, hot pad, table spoon

1.			
Margarine		2 tsp.	10 mL
Small onion, cut into thin rings		1	1
Wieners, cut into thin slices		2	2
2.	Hot dog buns, split open	2	2
	Condiments (such as prepared mustard, ketchup and sweet pickle relish), optional		

1. Melt the margarine in the frying pan on medium. Add the onion rings. Sauté for 3 minutes, stirring often, until the onion is soft. Add the wiener slices. Turn down the heat to low. Sauté, stirring occasionally, for about 6 minutes until the onion is golden. Remove the frying pan to the hot pad.

2. Spoon the mixture on the buns. Top with the mustard, ketchup and relish. Makes 2 onion dogs.

The onion really mellows and sweetens when cooked.

Make this delicious homemade version.

Creamy Macaroni & Cheese

GET READY ✔

measuring spoons, small saucepan, dry measures, 2 mixing spoons, liquid measures, hot pad, large saucepan, colander

1.	Margarine	1 tbsp.	15 mL
	Chopped onion	¼ cup	60 mL
2.	All-purpose flour	1½ tbsp.	25 mL
	Skim evaporated milk	1 cup	250 mL
	Grated Cheddar cheese	½ cup	125 mL
	Process Cheddar cheese slices	2	2
	Salt	¼ tsp.	1 mL
	Pepper, sprinkle		
	Dry mustard (or paprika)	¾ tsp.	4 mL
3.	Water	8 cups	2 L
	Elbow macaroni (or small shell pasta), uncooked	1 cup	250 mL

1. Melt the margarine in the small saucepan on medium. Sauté the onion until soft.

2. Stir in the flour. Gradually add the evaporated milk, stirring constantly, until boiling. Stir in both cheeses, salt, pepper and mustard. Stir until the cheeses are melted. Remove from the heat to the hot pad.

3. Measure the water into the large saucepan. Bring to a boil. Stir in the macaroni. Cook for 5 to 6 minutes until the macaroni is just tender. Drain in the colander. Return the macaroni to the saucepan. Add the cheese sauce. Stir well. Makes 4 cups (1 L).

Snappy Lunch

GET READY ✔

liquid measures, microwave-safe cereal bowl, measuring spoons, mixing spoon, oven mitts, hot pad

1.	Canned kidney beans	½ cup	125 mL
	Salsa	3 tbsp.	50 mL
2.	Grated Cheddar cheese	2 tbsp.	30 mL
	Grated mozzarella cheese	2 tbsp.	30 mL

1. Put the kidney beans into the bowl. Add the salsa. Stir.

2. Sprinkle with both cheeses. Microwave on high (100%) for about 2 minutes until the cheeses are melted. Use the oven mitts to remove the bowl to the hot pad. Serves 1.

An exceptionally good quick meal.

A very different taco.
Most enjoyable. Do
not freeze.

Tacos

GET READY ✔

non-stick frying pan, measuring spoons, dry measures, 5 small bowls

1.	Frozen breaded fish sticks	2	2
2.	Taco (or seafood) sauce	1 tbsp.	15 mL
	Chopped iceberg lettuce	¼ cup	60 mL
	Tomato slice, diced	1	1
	Grated Cheddar cheese	2 tbsp.	30 mL
	Sour cream (optional)	1 tbsp.	15 mL
3.	Taco shells	2	2

1. Heat the fish sticks in the frying pan on medium.

2. Put the next 5 ingredients into separate small bowls.

3. Place a fish stick in each taco shell. Layer the taco sauce, lettuce, tomato, cheese and sour cream over each fish stick. Makes 2 tacos.

Mexican Stir-Fry Sandwich

GET READY ✔

measuring spoons, frying pan, long-handled mixing spoon, dry measures, hot pad

1.	Cooking oil	1 tsp.	5 mL
	Boneless, skinless chicken breast half, slivered	1	1
2.	Garlic powder	⅛ tsp.	0.5 mL
	Salt	⅛ tsp.	0.5 mL
	Pepper	¹⁄₁₆ tsp.	0.5 mL
3.	Small red onion, thinly sliced	½	½
	Medium green pepper, slivered	1	1
	Salsa	⅓ cup	75 mL
4.	White (or whole-wheat) flour tortillas (10 inch, 25 cm, size)	3	3

Use medium or hot salsa if you want to make these spicier.

1. Heat the cooking oil in the frying pan on medium-high. Add the chicken. Stir-fry for 2 minutes.

2. Add the garlic powder, salt and pepper. Stir-fry for 2 minutes.

3. Add the red onion and green pepper to the chicken. Stir-fry for 3 minutes. Add the salsa. Stir-fry for 2 minutes until the vegetables are tender-crisp. Remove the frying pan to the hot pad. Makes 2 cups (500 mL) filling.

4. Divide the filling evenly among the tortillas. To roll, fold the bottom edge of the tortilla up over the chicken mixture to the centre. Fold the left side over the centre. Fold the right side overlapping the left side. Makes 3 rolled sandwiches.

Serve over toast, toasted bun halves, or inside slightly hollowed-out buns.

Easy Chili

 GET READY ✔
non-stick frying pan with lid, long-handled mixing spoon, measuring spoons

1.	Lean ground beef	1 lb.	454 g
	Medium onion, chopped	1	1
	Large celery rib, sliced	1	1
2.	All-purpose flour	2 tbsp.	30 mL
	Can of stewed tomatoes, with juice, chopped	14 oz.	398 mL
	Garlic powder	¼ tsp.	1 mL
	Can of kidney beans, drained	14 oz.	398 mL
	Chili powder	1 tbsp.	15 mL
	Granulated sugar	2 tsp.	10 mL
	Paprika	1 tsp.	5 mL
	Salt	½ tsp.	2 mL

1. Scramble-fry the ground beef, onion and celery in the frying pan on medium until the beef is no longer pink and the vegetables are tender-crisp.

2. Sprinkle the surface of the beef mixture with the flour. Stir for 1 minute. Add the remaining 7 ingredients. Bring to a boil. Place the lid on the frying pan. Simmer on low for 30 minutes, stirring several times. Makes 5¾ cups (1.45 L).

Chicken Pasta Casserole

GET READY ✔

liquid measures, dry measures, measuring spoons, large bowl, mixing spoon, 3 quart (3 L) casserole dish, oven mitts, wire rack

1.			
Can of condensed cream of mushroom soup	10 oz.	284 mL
Can of condensed cream of celery soup	10 oz.	284 mL
Water	2½ cups	625 mL
Grated Cheddar cheese	2 cups	500 mL
Diced cooked chicken (see Note)	2 cups	500 mL
Macaroni, uncooked	2 cups	500 mL
Diced onion	1 cup	250 mL
Salt	1 tsp.	5 mL
2. Shoestring potato chips	1 cup	250 mL

1. Mix the first 8 ingredients in the bowl. Turn into the ungreased casserole dish. Cover with the lid. Chill overnight.

2. Place the oven rack in the centre position. Turn the oven on to 350°F (175°C). Take the casserole dish from the refrigerator. Remove the lid. Sprinkle the potato chips over the top. Bake, uncovered, for 1 hour until the pasta is tender. Use the oven mitts to remove the casserole dish to the wire rack. Serves 6.

Note: If you don't have cooked chicken on hand, use two 6½ oz. (184 g) cans of flaked or chunk chicken, drained.

Make this the night before. Then all you have to do is put it into the oven the next day. The pasta is not precooked.

Ten of the juiciest meat servings ever. Just the right size to freeze. They are thin enough to thaw quickly.

Little Meat Muffins

GET READY ✔

medium bowl, mixing spoon, muffin pan (for 10 muffins), baking sheet, meat thermometer, oven mitts, wire rack

1.			
Lean ground beef	1 lb.	454 g
Can of condensed vegetable soup	10 oz.	284 mL

1. Place the oven rack in the centre position. Turn the oven on to 350°F (175°C). Mix the ground beef and soup in the bowl. Pack the beef mixture into 10 greased muffin cups. Set the muffin pan on the baking sheet to catch any drips. Bake for 40 to 45 minutes until meat thermometer inserted in the centre of a muffin reads 160°F (71°C). Use the oven mitts to remove the muffin pan to the wire rack. Let stand for 10 minutes before serving. Makes 10 meat muffins.

Chops are cooked with a dark sauce.

Pork Chops

GET READY ✔

measuring spoons, frying pan, pancake lifter, table fork, small roasting pan, dry measures, small bowl, mixing spoon, oven mitts, hot pad

1.	Cooking oil	1 tbsp.	15 mL
	Pork chops, trimmed of fat	6	6
2.	Chopped onion	1 cup	250 mL
3.	Ketchup	½ cup	125 mL
	Brown sugar, packed	¼ cup	60 mL
	White vinegar	3 tbsp.	50 mL
	Soy sauce	1 tbsp.	15 mL
	Salt	½ tsp.	2 mL
	Pepper	⅛ tsp.	0.5 mL

1. Place the oven rack in the centre position. Turn the oven on to 350°F (175°C). Heat the cooking oil in the frying pan on medium. Add the pork chops. Brown 1 side. Use the pancake lifter to turn the chops over. Brown. Use the fork to transfer the chops to the roasting pan.

2. Scatter the onion over the chops.

3. Measure the remaining 6 ingredients into the bowl. Stir. Pour over the chops and onion. Place the lid on the roasting pan. Bake for about 1 hour until the meat is tender. Use the oven mitts to remove the roasting pan to the hot pad. Serves 6.

Stroganoff

1.	Cooking oil	1 tbsp.	15 mL
	Lean ground beef	1 lb.	454 g
2.	Can of condensed cream of mushroom soup	10 oz.	284 mL
	Water	1 cup	250 mL
	Envelope of dry onion soup mix	1¼ oz.	38 g
	Medium noodles, uncooked	1 cup	250 mL
	Can of sliced mushrooms, drained	10 oz.	284 mL
	Ketchup	1 tbsp.	15 mL
3.	Sour cream	½ cup	125 mL
	Process cheese slice, broken up	1	1

1. Heat the cooking oil in the frying pan on medium. Add the ground beef. Scramble-fry until the meat is browned and crumbly.

2. Add the next 6 ingredients to the beef. Stir. Place the lid on the frying pan. Simmer on low for about 10 minutes until the pasta is tender but firm. Remove the lid.

3. Add the sour cream and cheese. Stir until the cheese melts. Serves 4.

Add a salad and a vegetable and you're all set. The pasta is added raw.

These might look like cinnamon rolls, but they have a great pizza flavour.

Pizza Pinwheels

GET READY ✔

baking sheet, dry measures, liquid measures, medium bowl, mixing spoon, rolling pin, ruler, measuring spoons, small bowl, sharp knife, cutting board, oven mitts, wire rack

1.			
	Biscuit mix	2¼ cups	560 mL
	Water	½ cup	125 mL
	Biscuit mix, as needed, to prevent sticking		
2.	Can of pizza sauce	7½ oz.	213 mL
	Green onions, sliced	2	2
	Finely chopped green pepper	½ cup	125 mL
	Finely chopped pepperoni	½ cup	125 mL
	Grated mozzarella cheese	1 cup	250 mL
	Dried whole oregano	¼ tsp.	1 mL

1. Place the oven rack in the centre position. Turn the oven on to 400°F (205°C). Grease the baking sheet. Stir the biscuit mix and water in the medium bowl until the dough starts to form a ball. Turn the dough out onto the counter that has been lightly dusted with more biscuit mix. Gently knead the dough 20 times. Dust the dough with the biscuit mix and roll out to a 12 × 12 inch (30 × 30 cm) square.

2. Combine the remaining 6 ingredients in the small bowl. Mix well. Spread over the dough, leaving about 1 inch (2.5 cm) all around the outside edge. Roll up the dough from 1 side to the other like a jelly roll. Pinch along the long edge of the roll to seal. Cut into twelve 1 inch (2.5 cm) thick slices on the cutting board. Place the slices on the baking sheet. Bake in the oven for 12 minutes. Use the oven mitts to remove the baking sheet to the wire rack. Makes 12 pinwheels.

Hot Tortilla Dip

GET READY ✔

dry measures, small microwave-safe bowl, sharp knife, cutting board, paper towel, mixing spoon, measuring spoons, plastic wrap, oven mitts, hot pad

1.	Chunky salsa	½ cup	125 mL
	Small tomato	1	1
2.	Green onion, thinly sliced	1	1
	Dried crushed chilies	⅛ tsp.	0.5 mL
3.	Process cheese loaf (such as Velveeta), cut into small cubes	4 oz.	125 g

1. Measure the salsa into the bowl. Cut the tomato in half on the cutting board. Gently squeeze the tomato over the paper towel to remove the seeds. Discard the seeds and juice. Dice the tomato into small pieces on the cutting board. Stir into the salsa.

2. Add the green onion and crushed chilies. Cover loosely with plastic wrap. Microwave on high (100%) for 1 minute.

3. Stir the cheese into the warm salsa mixture. Microwave, uncovered, on high (100%) for 30 seconds. Stir well. Repeat until the cheese is melted. Use the oven mitts to remove the bowl to the hot pad. Makes 1¼ cups (300 mL).

Make this ahead and keep chilled. Reheat for lunch!

Rarebit Wieners

GET READY ✔
baking sheet, dry measures, measuring spoons, small bowl, mixing spoon, table knife, oven mitts, wire rack

1.	Hamburger buns, split and lightly toasted	2	2
2.	Wieners, sliced	2	2
	Grated Cheddar cheese	½ cup	125 mL
	Dry mustard	½ tsp.	2 mL
	Ketchup	1 tbsp.	15 mL
	Salad dressing (or mayonnaise)	1 tbsp.	15 mL
3.	Paprika, sprinkle		

Lots of hot dog taste!

1. Place the oven rack in the centre position. Turn the oven on to 350°F (175°C). Place the bun halves, toasted side up, on the ungreased baking sheet.

2. Mix the next 5 ingredients in the bowl. Divide the mixture among the 4 bun halves. Pack down with the table knife to cover to the edge of the buns.

3. Sprinkle lightly with the paprika. Bake in the oven for 15 minutes until the tops are bubbly and starting to brown. Use the oven mitts to remove the baking sheet to the wire rack. Makes 4 bun halves.

Great dip for nacho chips, veggies or bread. Just like a fondue.

Hot Mushroom Cheddar Dip

GET READY ✔

liquid measures, dry measures, measuring spoons, medium microwave-safe bowl, mixing spoon

1.	Can of condensed cream of mushroom soup	10 oz.	284 mL
	Skim evaporated milk	¾ cup	175 mL
	Grated Cheddar cheese	2 cups	500 mL
	Worcestershire sauce	1 tsp.	5 mL
2.	Green onion, sliced	1	1

1. Combine the first 4 ingredients in the bowl. Stir. Microwave, uncovered, on high (100%) for 2 to 3 minutes. Stir well. Microwave, uncovered, on high (100%) for 30 seconds until the cheese is melted.

2. Sprinkle with the green onion. Makes 2 cups (500 mL).

For spicy nachos, add some chilies. Use one or both of the cheeses. Do not freeze.

Nachos

GET READY ✔
baking sheet, dry measures, oven mitts, wire rack

1.	Tortilla chips	2 oz.	57 g
2.	Grated Cheddar cheese	⅓ cup	75 mL
	Grated Monterey Jack cheese	⅓ cup	75 mL
	Green onion, thinly sliced	1	1
	Green or ripe olives, sliced	4	4
3.	Salsa	¼ cup	60 mL
	Sour cream	¼ cup	60 mL

1. Place the oven rack in the centre position. Turn the oven on to 350°F (175°C). Crowd the tortilla chips on the ungreased baking sheet.

2. Sprinkle with both cheeses, green onion and olive slices. Bake in the oven for about 3 minutes until the cheeses are melted. Use the oven mitts to remove the baking sheet to the wire rack.

3. Serve with the salsa and sour cream on the side. Serves 1.

Jiffy Pizza

GET READY ✔

frying pan, paper towel, sharp knife, cutting board, measuring spoons, small cup, small mixing spoon, baking sheet, table knife, oven mitts, wire rack

1.	Bacon slices	2	2
2.	Ketchup	2 tbsp.	30 mL
	Dried whole oregano	¼ tsp.	1 mL
	Onion powder	¼ tsp.	1 mL
3.	Hamburger bun, split and buttered	1	1
4.	Process cheese slices	2	2
	Mozzarella cheese slices	2	2

1. Place the oven rack in the top position. Turn the oven on to broil. Fry the bacon in the frying pan on medium-low until cooked but not crisp. Drain on the paper towel. Cut the slices into small pieces on the cutting board.

2. Stir the ketchup, oregano and onion powder in the small cup.

3. Place the 2 bun halves on the baking sheet. Spread the ketchup mixture with the table knife over the 2 bun halves.

4. Lay the cheese slices over the ketchup mixture. Sprinkle the bacon on the cheese. Broil in the oven for 1 to 2 minutes until the cheeses are melted. Watch carefully so that they don't burn. Use the oven mitts to remove the baking sheet to the wire rack. Serves 1.

A good quick pizza snack.

The next best thing to visiting Hawaii.

Hawaiian Grilled Cheese

GET READY ✔

non-stick frying pan, measuring spoons, table knife, pancake lifter, small plate

1.			
Margarine	2 tsp.	10 mL
White (or whole-wheat) bread slices	2	2
Process cheese slices	2	2
Ham slice (1 oz., 28 g)	1	1
Pineapple slice, blotted very dry with paper towel	1	1

1. Heat the frying pan on medium-low. Spread the margarine on 1 side of each bread slice. Place 1 slice of cheese on the unbuttered side of each slice. Layer the ham and pineapple. Place the second slice of bread, buttered side up, on top. Set the sandwich in the frying pan. When the bottom side is browned, use the pancake lifter to turn the sandwich over. Brown the other side. Use the lifter to remove the sandwich to the plate. Makes 1 sandwich.

Pita Pizza

GET READY ✔
baking sheet, measuring spoons, dry measures, oven mitts, wire rack

1.	Pita bread (8 inch, 20 cm, size)	1	1
2.	Pizza (or spaghetti) sauce	2 tbsp.	30 mL
3.	Chopped cooked ham	2 tbsp.	30 mL
	Whole fresh mushrooms, chopped	2	2
	Grated mozzarella cheese	⅓ cup	75 mL
	Diced green pepper	2 tbsp.	30 mL

1. Place the oven rack in the top position. Turn the oven on to broil. Place the pita bread on the ungreased baking sheet. Flatten with your hand.

2. Spread the pizza sauce over the pita almost to the edge, using the back of the measuring spoon.

3. Sprinkle the ham, mushrooms, cheese and green pepper over the sauce. Broil in the oven for about 7 minutes until the cheese is melted and the edge of the pita is crisp. Use the oven mitts to remove the baking sheet to the wire rack to cool. Cuts into 6 wedges.

If you like a thin-crust pizza this is the one for you.

Pizza Pop-Ups

GET READY ✔

muffin pan (for 10 muffins), liquid measures, dry measures, measuring spoons, medium bowl, mixing spoon, oven mitts, wire rack

1.			
Tomato sauce	½ cup	125 mL
Chopped pepperoni	1 cup	250 mL
Finely chopped onion	1 tbsp.	15 mL
Grated Parmesan cheese	1 tbsp.	15 mL
Grated mozzarella cheese	½ cup	125 mL
2. Refrigerator flaky rolls (10 per tube)	12 oz.	340 g

1. Place the oven rack in the centre position. Turn the oven on to 350°F (175°C). Grease the muffin pan. Mix the first 5 ingredients in the bowl.

2. Divide each roll in half. Place 1 piece of the dough in the bottom of each of the 10 muffin cups. Push down with your finger to form a shell. If the dough sticks to your finger, coat your finger with flour. Divide the pepperoni mixture among the 10 shells. Slightly flatten the remaining 10 pieces of the dough. Place over the pepperoni mixture. Push the edges down to seal. Bake in the oven for 15 to 20 minutes until golden. Use the oven mitts to remove the pan to the wire rack to cool. Makes 10 pop-ups.

Perfect for after basketball practice or video movie night.

These have a great nacho kick to them.

Nacho Potato Chunks

GET READY ✔

9 x 9 inch (22 x 22 cm) square baking pan, sharp knife, cutting board, small bowl, measuring spoons, mixing spoon, oven mitts, wire rack

1.	Unpeeled medium potatoes	2	2
2.	Cooking oil	1 tbsp.	15 mL
	Taco seasoning mix (from envelope)	2 tbsp.	30 mL
	Sour cream, for dipping		

1. Place the oven rack in the centre position. Turn the oven on to 450°F (230°C). Grease the pan. Slice the potatoes in half lengthwise on the cutting board. Slice each half crosswise into 4 pieces to make 8 chunks for each potato. Place in the bowl.

2. Drizzle the cooking oil over the potato chunks. Sprinkle with the taco seasoning. Stir to coat well. Spread the potato in a single layer in the pan. Bake in the oven for 15 minutes. Use the oven mitts to remove the pan to the wire rack. Turn down the oven temperature to 400°F (205°C). Stir the potato chunks. Spread out. Bake for 15 minutes. Use the oven mitts to remove the pan to the wire rack to cool. Serve with the sour cream. Serves 2.

Variation: Sprinkle with ½ cup (125 mL) grated Cheddar or Monterey Jack cheese before the last baking time.

Serve with hamburgers or on its own as a meal. Do not freeze.

Taco Salad

GET READY ✔

dry measures, large bowl, small spoon, sharp knife, cutting board, liquid measures, measuring spoons, small bowl, small mixing spoon, pair of salad tongs (or 2 spoons)

1.			
	Chopped iceberg lettuce	4 cups	1 L
	Grated Cheddar cheese	1 cup	250 mL
	Can of kidney beans, drained	14 oz.	398 mL
	Large tomato, halved	1	1
	Green onions, sliced	4	4
2.	Salad dressing (or mayonnaise)	½ cup	125 mL
	Taco seasoning mix (from envelope)	2 tbsp.	30 mL
3.	Tortilla chips, broken up	8 oz.	225 g

1. Put the lettuce, cheese and kidney beans into the large bowl. Squeeze each tomato half to remove the juice. Use the small spoon to remove the seeds. Discard the juice and seeds. Dice the tomato on the cutting board. Add the tomato and green onion to the lettuce mixture.

2. Stir the salad dressing and taco seasoning in the small bowl. Pour over the salad. Use the salad tongs to toss and coat the lettuce mixture with the dressing.

3. Add the tortilla chips just before serving. If added too soon they will get soggy. Makes 8 side salads.

Almost like the adult version but so quick and easy. Make it for the whole family. Do not freeze.

Caesar Salad

GET READY ✔

measuring spoons, small bowl, mixing spoon, large bowl, dry measures, pair of salad tongs (or 2 spoons)

1. **DRESSING**

White vinegar	2 tbsp.	30 mL
Water	2 tbsp.	30 mL
Cooking oil	2 tsp.	10 mL
Granulated sugar	2 tsp.	10 mL
Prepared mustard	½ tsp.	2 mL
Garlic powder	¼ tsp.	1 mL

2.

Head of romaine lettuce	1	1
Croutons	1½ cups	375 mL
Grated Parmesan cheese	½ cup	125 mL
Large hard-boiled eggs, chopped	2	2

1. **Dressing:** Combine the first 6 ingredients in the small bowl. Stir well.

2. Wash and dry the lettuce. Tear into bite-size pieces. Put the lettuce into the large bowl. Add the croutons, cheese and egg. Pour the dressing over the lettuce mixture. Use the salad tongs to toss and coat the lettuce with the dressing. Serves 6.

Coconut Marshmallow Salad

GET READY ✔

dry measures, large bowl, mixing spoon, rubber spatula, plastic wrap

1.			
Miniature coloured marshmallows	1 cup	250 mL
Can of fruit cocktail, well drained	14 oz.	398 mL
Can of mandarin oranges, well		
drained	10 oz.	284 mL
Long thread white or coloured coconut	½ cup	125 mL
(optional)		
Maraschino cherries, halved	6	6
2. Sour cream (or plain yogurt)	1 cup	250 mL

1. Combine the marshmallows, drained fruits, coconut and cherries in the bowl. Stir.

2. Fold in the sour cream using the spatula. Cover the bowl with plastic wrap. Chill for 30 minutes to allow the flavours to blend and the marshmallows to soften. Makes 4 cups (1 L).

A showy rainbow of colour.

Cottage cheese and peaches served on a bed of crisp lettuce.

Peaches 'N' Cream Salad

GET READY ✔

salad bowl (or salad plate), dry measures, small spoon, measuring spoons

1.	Shredded crisp iceberg lettuce (handful)		
2.	Creamed cottage cheese	½ cup	125 mL
3.	Can of sliced peaches, juice reserved	14 oz.	398 mL
	Reserved peach juice	1 tbsp.	15 mL
	Maraschino cherry, for garnish	1	1

1. Put the lettuce into the bowl or onto the plate.

2. Spoon the cottage cheese into the middle of the bed of lettuce.

3. Arrange the peach slices around the cottage cheese. Drizzle the peach juice over all. Top with the cherry. Serves 1.

FRUIT 'N' CREAM SALAD: Use canned fruit cocktail instead of the peaches.

JAM 'N' CREAM SALAD: Use 1 tbsp. (15 mL) jam on top if you don't have any fruit.

Apple Grape Salad

dry measures, medium bowl, 2 mixing spoons, measuring spoons, small bowl

1.	Red or green seedless grapes, halved	10	10
	Chopped walnuts (optional)	¼ cup	60 mL
	Thinly sliced celery	¼ cup	60 mL
	Small apple, cored and chopped	1	1
2.	Salad dressing (or mayonnaise)	2 tbsp.	30 mL
	Granulated sugar	1 tsp.	5 mL
	Lemon juice	1 tsp.	5 mL

1. Mix the first 4 ingredients in the medium bowl.

2. Stir the remaining 3 ingredients in the small bowl. Pour over the fruit mixture. Toss to coat. Makes 1½ cups (375 mL).

Crunchy but not too sweet. You'll give this a thumbs up!

For kids of all ages. Tasty. Do not freeze.

Carrot Raisin Salad

GET READY ✔

dry measures, medium bowl, mixing spoon, liquid measures, measuring spoons, small bowl

1.	Grated carrot (2-3 medium)	2 cups	500 mL
	Raisins	½ cup	125 mL
	Canned crushed pineapple, drained	½ cup	125 mL
2.	Salad dressing (or mayonnaise)	⅓ cup	75 mL
	White vinegar	2 tsp.	10 mL
	Granulated sugar	2 tsp.	10 mL

1. Combine the carrot, raisins and pineapple in the medium bowl. Stir.

2. Measure the salad dressing, vinegar and sugar into the small bowl. Stir. Pour over the carrot mixture. Stir to coat. Makes about 2 cups (500 mL).

Corn Chowder

1.	Bacon slices, diced	2	2
2.	Chopped onion	¼ cup	60 mL
	Chopped green or red pepper	¼ cup	60 mL
	All-purpose flour	1 tbsp.	15 mL
	Milk	1 cup	250 mL
	Can of cream-style corn	14 oz.	398 mL
3.	Parsley flakes	1 tsp.	5 mL
	Hot pepper sauce, dash		
	Pepper, sprinkle		

1. Fry the bacon in the saucepan on medium until crisp. Do not drain.

2. Add the onion and green pepper. Sauté for 2 minutes until soft. Sprinkle the flour over the vegetables. Stir well. Slowly add the milk and corn, stirring constantly, until the mixture comes to a simmer. Remove the saucepan to the hot pad.

3. Add the remaining 3 ingredients. Stir. Makes 3 cups (750 mL).

This delicious chowder is made from canned cream-style corn.

Easy Macaroni Soup

GET READY ✔

liquid measures, measuring spoons, large saucepan, mixing spoon, dry measures, small bowl

1.	Water	4 cups	1 L
	Seasoned salt	½ tsp.	2 mL
	Package of macaroni and cheese dinner, cheese-flavoured packet reserved	6½ oz.	200 g
2.	Frozen mixed vegetables	1 cup	250 mL
	Condensed chicken broth	10 oz.	284 mL
	Onion powder	1 tsp.	5 mL
	Pepper, sprinkle		
3.	All-purpose flour	2 tbsp.	30 mL
	Reserved cheese-flavoured packet		
	Milk	1 cup	250 mL

1. Bring the water and seasoned salt to a boil in the saucepan. Add only the macaroni from the package. Boil for 5 minutes, stirring occasionally.

2. Add the vegetables, chicken broth, onion powder and pepper. Return to a boil. Cook for 5 minutes until the macaroni is tender.

3. Combine the flour and cheese-flavoured packet in the bowl. Slowly add the milk, stirring constantly, until smooth. Add to the macaroni and vegetables in the saucepan. Cook, stirring constantly, for 2 or 3 minutes until heated through. Makes 7 cups (1.75 L).

If you like macaroni and cheese, you will want to try this recipe.

Easy to assemble and cook.

Chicken Barley Soup

GET READY ✔

liquid measures, measuring spoons, dry measures, large saucepan, mixing spoon, hot pad

1.			
Water	5 cups	1.25 L
Chicken bouillon powder	5 tsp.	25 mL
Diced carrot	½ cup	125 mL
Diced potato	½ cup	125 mL
Diced onion	½ cup	125 mL
Pearl barley	½ cup	125 mL
Can of tomatoes, with juice, broken up	14 oz.	398 mL
2. Can of flaked chicken (or turkey)	6½ oz.	184 g

1. Combine the first 7 ingredients in the saucepan. Stir. Heat on medium-high, stirring often, until the mixture comes to a boil. Place the lid on the saucepan. Turn down the heat to medium-low. Simmer, stirring occasionally, for about 1 hour.

2. Add the chicken. Simmer to heat through. Remove the saucepan to the hot pad. Makes 6½ cups (1.6 L).

Bean 'N' Bacon Soup

GET READY ✔

large saucepan, long-handled mixing spoon, colander, liquid measures, measuring spoons, hot pad

1.	Bacon slices, diced	2	2
	Small onion, chopped	1	1
2.	Large potato, diced	1	1
	Water	2 cups	500 mL
3.	Can of condensed vegetable soup	10 oz.	284 mL
	Can of beans in tomato sauce, mashed with a fork	14 oz.	398 mL
	Hot pepper sauce, dash	1/8-1/4 tsp.	0.5-1 mL
4.	Grated Cheddar cheese, for garnish		

1. Fry the bacon in the saucepan on medium for 2 minutes. Add the onion. Stir. Sauté for about 5 minutes until the bacon is cooked and the onion is soft. Drain in the colander.

2. Add the potato and water. Bring the mixture to a boil. Place the lid on the saucepan. Simmer for 10 to 12 minutes until the potato is tender.

3. Add the vegetable soup, beans and hot pepper sauce. Simmer, uncovered, for 10 minutes. Stir occasionally. Remove the saucepan to the hot pad.

4. Garnish individual servings with the cheese. Makes 5½ cups (1.4 L).

Add more hot pepper sauce to make as zippy as you want.

You'll have fun making these. You can change the flavour of these little peanut butter balls just by rolling them in a different coating.

Peanut Butter Candy

GET READY ✓

dry measures, medium bowl, measuring spoons, mixing spoon, small bowl, covered container

1.	Smooth or crunchy peanut butter	⅔ cup	150 mL
	Granola cereal	¾ cup	175 mL
	Skim milk powder	⅓ cup	75 mL
	Brown sugar, packed	1 tbsp.	15 mL
2.	Mini semisweet or multi-coloured chocolate baking chips	½ cup	125 mL
3.	Graham cracker (or chocolate wafer) crumbs, chocolate sprinkles or fine coconut, for coating	½ cup	125 mL

1. Put the peanut butter into the medium bowl. Add the cereal, milk powder and brown sugar. Mix with your hands.

2. Add the chocolate chips. Mix well. Shape the dough into 1 inch (2.5 cm) balls.

3. Place your choice of coating in the small bowl. Roll the balls in the coating. Place in a covered container. Chill. Makes 28 balls.

Toasted Coconut Mallows

GET READY ✔

dry measures, 9 × 9 inch (22 × 22 cm) square baking pan, oven mitts, hot pad, mixing spoon, small bowl, liquid measures, large saucepan, long-handled barbecue fork, paper towel, waxed paper

1.	Medium coconut	1 cup	250 mL
2.	Water	4-6 cups	1-1.5 L
3.	Large white or coloured marshmallows	30	30

1. Place the oven rack in the centre position. Turn the oven on to 350°F (175°C). Spread the coconut in the ungreased pan in an even layer. Bake in the oven for 6 minutes, removing with the oven mitts to the hot pad every 2 minutes to stir, until golden. Cool. Transfer to the bowl.

2. Put the water into the saucepan. Bring to a boil. Turn down the heat to medium.

3. Use the barbecue fork to dip each marshmallow quickly into the boiling water. Dab the marshmallow on the paper towel. Remove the marshmallow from the fork. Roll in the coconut. Set on the waxed paper to firm. Makes 30 marshmallow treats.

Impress your friends with these.

Cone Cupcakes

GET READY ✔

dry measures, medium bowl, electric mixer, measuring spoons, small bowl, mixing spoon, liquid measures, large table spoon, baking sheet, wooden toothpick

1.	Hard margarine, softened	½ cup	125 mL
	Granulated sugar	1 cup	250 mL
	Large eggs	2	2
	Vanilla flavouring	1 tsp.	5 mL
2.	All-purpose flour	1¾ cups	425 mL
	Baking powder	2½ tsp.	12 mL
	Salt	¼ tsp.	1 mL
3.	Milk	⅔ cup	150 mL
4.	Flat-bottomed ice-cream cones	24	24

1. Place the oven rack in the centre position. Turn the oven on to 375°F (190°C). Cream the margarine and sugar well in the medium bowl on medium with the mixer. Beat in the eggs, 1 at a time, on high. Mix in the vanilla flavouring.

2. Measure the flour, baking powder and salt into the small bowl. Stir.

3. Add the milk to the margarine mixture in 2 parts, alternately with the flour mixture in 3 parts, beginning and ending with the flour mixture.

4. Spoon the batter into the cones to within ½ inch (12 mm) of the top. Set the filled cones on the baking sheet. Bake in the oven for 15 to 20 minutes until the wooden toothpick inserted in the centre of each cone comes out clean. Makes 24 cupcakes.

Make for your friends or even your parents. Ice with your favorite coloured icing.

Just bursting with colour. Kids will love it. Best eaten the same day it is made.

Popcorn Cake

GET READY ✔

dry measures, large heavy saucepan, long-handled mixing spoon, very large bowl, 10 inch (25 cm) tube pan

1.	Hard margarine	1 cup	250 mL
	Large marshmallows	32	32
2.	Popped popcorn (about ¾ cup, 175 mL, kernels)	16 cups	4 L
3.	Small gumdrops (no black)	1 cup	250 mL
	Chocolate-covered peanuts	1 cup	250 mL
	Candy-coated chocolate candies	1 cup	250 mL

1. Melt the margarine and marshmallows in the saucepan on low, stirring often.

2. Put the popped popcorn into the bowl. Pour the hot marshmallow mixture over the top. Quickly stir before the mixture starts to harden.

3. Quickly add the remaining 3 ingredients. Mix well. Pack into the greased tube pan. Cool completely. Cuts into 12 wedges.

Snowballs

GET READY ✔

dry measures, large saucepan, liquid measures, measuring spoons, long-handled mixing spoon, hot pad, small bowl, waxed paper, covered container

1.	Hard margarine	½ cup	125 mL
	Chopped pitted dates	2 cups	500 mL
	Water	¼ cup	60 mL
	Ground cinnamon	⅛ tsp.	0.5 mL
2.	Chopped walnuts (or pecans), optional	½ cup	125 mL
	Granola cereal	½ cup	125 mL
	Crisp rice cereal	½ cup	125 mL
3.	Flake coconut	¾ cup	175 mL

Crunchy and sweet. Made with granola and crisp rice cereal.

1. Melt the margarine in the saucepan on medium. Add the dates, water and cinnamon. Stir. Heat until the mixture comes to a boil. Turn down the heat to low. Heat, stirring constantly, for 5 minutes until the mixture is thickened. Remove the saucepan to the hot pad. Cool for 10 minutes.

2. Add the walnuts, granola cereal and rice cereal. Mix well.

3. Put the coconut into the small bowl. Wet your hands with water. Shape the cereal mixture into 1 inch (2.5 cm) balls. Roll the balls in the coconut. Place on the waxed paper on the counter or chill in a covered container. Serve at room temperature or chilled. Makes 30 balls.

Marshmallow Nests

GET READY ✔

dry measures, medium microwave-safe bowl, mixing spoon, table spoon, waxed paper

1.	Smooth peanut butter	1 cup	250 mL
	Semisweet chocolate chips	1 cup	250 mL
2.	Large shredded wheat cereal biscuits	6	6
	Miniature white or coloured marshmallows	60	60

1. Put the peanut butter and chocolate chips into the bowl. Microwave, uncovered, on high (100%) for 1 minute. Stir. Microwave, uncovered, on high (100%) for 1 minute. Stir to melt the chocolate chips.

2. Crumble the wheat cereal biscuits into the chocolate mixture. Stir until well coated. Drop by spoonfuls onto the waxed paper. Push 3 marshmallows into the middle of each to form a "nest with its eggs." Cool completely. Makes 20 nests.

These would make a great treat on Easter Sunday.

Sweet and a bit gooey inside. Freeze any extras.

Apple Pockets

GET READY ✔

two 8 inch (20 cm) round cake pans, measuring spoons, small bowl, mixing spoon, oven mitts, wire racks, dry measures, small sealable plastic bag, scissors

1.	Tubes of refrigerator crescent-style rolls (8½ oz., 235 g, each)	2	2
2.	Small apple, peeled, cored and finely diced	1	1
	Granulated sugar	2 tbsp.	30 mL
	Ground cinnamon	½ tsp.	2 mL
3.	Icing (confectioner's) sugar	½ cup	125 mL
	Vanilla flavouring	½ tsp.	2 mL
	Milk	1 tbsp.	15 mL

1. Place the oven rack in the centre position. Turn the oven on to 375°F (190°C). Grease the cake pans. Open the crescent rolls and separate into 16 triangles.

2. Combine the next 3 ingredients in the bowl. Mix well. Drop a small spoonful of the apple mixture near the wide end of each triangle. Fold the long points toward the middle over the top of the filling. Pinch to seal. Fold over to the third point. Pinch to seal. Place, seam-side down, in each cake pan, 8 per pan. Bake in the oven for 12 minutes until golden. Use the oven mitts to remove the cake pans to the wire racks.

3. Combine the icing sugar, vanilla flavouring and milk in the plastic bag. Squeeze out the air. Seal. Squish the bag to mix the ingredients until smooth. Make a tiny cut across 1 corner with the scissors. Squeeze a zigzag pattern over each pastry. Makes 16 pockets.

Just like the ones you get in a fast-food restaurant—only better!

Chili Fries

GET READY ✔

non-stick frying pan, dry measures, long-handled mixing spoon, measuring spoons, liquid measures, baking sheet, oven mitts, wire rack

1.	Lean ground beef	1 lb.	454 g
	Chopped onion	1 cup	250 mL
	Finely chopped celery	2 cups	500 mL
2.	All-purpose flour	1 tbsp.	15 mL
	Can of kidney beans, drained	14 oz.	398 mL
	Seasoned salt	1 tsp.	5 mL
	Pepper	⅛ tsp.	0.5 mL
	Chili powder	1½ tsp.	7 mL
	Can of tomato sauce	7½ oz.	213 mL
	Ketchup	¼ cup	60 mL
3.	Frozen french fries	4 cups	1 L

1. Place the oven rack in the centre position. Turn the oven on to 425°F (220°C). Scramble-fry the ground beef in the frying pan on medium for 3 minutes with the long-handled mixing spoon. Add the onion and celery. Scramble-fry until the beef is no longer pink and the onion is soft.

2. Sprinkle with the flour. Stir well. Add the next 6 ingredients. Mix well. Bring to a boil. Pour into the ungreased baking sheet.

3. Top with the french fries. Bake in the oven for 25 to 30 minutes. Use the oven mitts to remove the baking sheet to the wire rack. Serves 6.

Carrot Combo

GET READY ✔

liquid measures, medium saucepan, dry measures, measuring spoons, sharp knife, colander, hot pad, potato masher

1. **Water**

Sliced carrot	3 cups	750 mL
Cubed yellow turnip	1 cup	250 mL
Salt	½ tsp.	2 mL
Granulated sugar	½ tsp.	2 mL

1. Pour enough water into the saucepan to be 1 inch (2.5 cm) deep. Add the carrot, turnip, salt and sugar. Place the lid on the saucepan. Bring to a boil on medium-high. Turn down the heat to medium-low. Simmer for about 20 minutes until the knife can easily pierce the vegetables. Drain in the colander. Return to the saucepan. Set the saucepan on the hot pad. Mash well. Serves 4.

Pictured on page 195.

Saucy Corn

GET READY ✔

measuring spoons, medium saucepan, mixing spoon, liquid measures, hot pad

1. **Margarine**

Margarine	2 tbsp.	30 mL
All-purpose flour	2 tbsp.	30 mL
Salt	½ tsp.	2 mL
Pepper	⅛ tsp.	0.5 mL
Milk	1 cup	250 mL

2. **Can of kernel corn, drained**

Can of kernel corn, drained	12 oz.	341 mL
Finely chopped green pepper	1 tbsp.	15 mL
Finely chopped pimiento	1 tbsp.	15 mL

1. Melt the margarine in the saucepan. Mix in the flour, salt and pepper. Add the milk. Stir until the mixture is boiling and thickened.

2. Add the remaining 3 ingredients. Stir to heat through. Remove the saucepan to the hot pad. Serves 4.

Pictured on page 195.

Creamy Peas

GET READY ✔

dry measures, liquid measures, measuring spoons, small saucepan, mixing spoon, colander, hot pad

1.	Frozen peas	2½ cups	625 mL
	Water	½ cup	125 mL
	Chicken bouillon powder	½ tsp.	2 mL
2.	Sour cream	¼ cup	60 mL
	Salt, sprinkle		
	Pepper, sprinkle		

1. Combine the frozen peas, water and bouillon powder in the saucepan. Stir. Place the lid on the saucepan. Bring to a boil on medium. Turn down the heat to medium-low. Simmer for 3 minutes. Drain well.

2. Add the sour cream, salt and pepper. Stir to coat the peas. Return the saucepan to the burner. Heat through on low. Remove the saucepan to the hot pad. Makes 4 servings.

Carrot Combo, page 194, shown at the top, is made with turnips and carrots. Saucy Corn, page 194, bottom left, will make a colourful addition to any meal. Creamy Peas, above, shown bottom right, are a snap to make.

Flavourful Rice

GET READY ✔

dry measures, measuring spoons, liquid measures, medium saucepan,
long-handled mixing spoon, small saucepan, colander

1.			
Long grain white rice	1 cup	250 mL
Chopped onion	½ cup	125 mL
Chicken bouillon powder	1 tsp.	5 mL
Water	2 cups	500 mL
Salt	½ tsp.	2 mL
2.			
Water	½ cup	125 mL
Frozen peas	1 cup	250 mL

1. Combine the first 5 ingredients in the medium saucepan. Stir. Place the lid on the saucepan. Bring the mixture to a boil on medium-high. Stir. Turn down the heat to medium-low. Simmer for 15 minutes until the rice is tender and the water is absorbed. Do not lift the lid while the rice is cooking.

2. Measure the second amount of water and frozen peas into the small saucepan. Place the lid on the saucepan. Bring to a boil on medium-high. Turn down the heat to medium-low. Simmer for 3 minutes. Drain in the colander. Stir the peas into the rice. Serves 4.

This rice is easy to make.
The peas add a burst
of colour to this
flavourful rice.

Mushroom Swiss Potato

GET READY ✔

table fork, paper towel, oven mitts, cutting board, measuring spoons, frying pan, mixing spoon, hot pad, sharp knife, small microwave-safe bowl, table spoon

1.	Unpeeled large potato	1	1
2.	Margarine	2 tsp.	10 mL
	Large whole fresh mushrooms, sliced	4	4
3.	Garlic powder, sprinkle		
	Salt, sprinkle		
	Pepper, sprinkle		
4.	Process Swiss cheese slice, cut into pieces	1	1

1. Wash the potato well. Poke 3 or 4 times with the fork. Wrap in the paper towel. Microwave on high (100%) for 7 minutes. Use the oven mitts to remove the potato to the cutting board.

2. Melt the margarine in the frying pan on medium. Add the mushrooms. Sauté for 1 minute.

3. Add the next 3 ingredients. Sauté until the mushrooms are golden. Remove the frying pan to the hot pad.

4. Cut a large X in the top of the potato, about 1 inch (2.5 cm) deep. Push the bottom sides inward to open the X slightly. Place the potato on the plate. Lay the pieces of cheese in the X. Spoon the mushrooms over the top. Microwave on high (100%) for 30 seconds to melt the cheese. Makes 1 large stuffed potato.

A hearty stuffed potato that is quick to make and nutritious.

Broccoli-Sauced Potatoes

GET READY ✔

table fork, measuring spoons, sharp knife, oven mitts, cutting board, dry measures, liquid measures, medium saucepan, colander, small bowl, hot pad, mixing spoon, 8 medium plates

1.	Unpeeled medium potatoes	4	4
	Cooking oil	1 tsp.	5 mL
2.	Chopped fresh (or frozen) broccoli	2 cups	500 mL
	Water	½ cup	125 mL
3.	Margarine	2 tbsp.	30 mL
	Chopped onion	¼ cup	60 mL
	All-purpose flour	3 tbsp.	50 mL
	Milk	1 cup	250 mL
4.	Process Swiss cheese slices, cut into small pieces	4	4
	Ground nutmeg, sprinkle		
	Seasoned salt	½ tsp.	2 mL
	Pepper, sprinkle		

1. Place the oven rack in the centre position. Turn the oven on to 425°F (220°C). Wash the potatoes well. Poke 3 or 4 times with the fork. Coat your hands with the cooking oil and rub the potatoes all over. Bake in the oven for 45 to 50 minutes until tender when pierced with the knife. Use the oven mitts to remove the potatoes to the cutting board.

2. Put the broccoli into the water in the saucepan. Bring to a boil on medium-high. Turn down the heat to medium-low. Place the lid on the saucepan. Simmer for 5 minutes until tender. Drain the broccoli well in the colander. Place the broccoli in the bowl. Set on the hot pad.

3. Melt the margarine in the same saucepan on medium. Sauté the onion until soft. Sprinkle the flour over the onion. Mix well. Gradually add the milk, stirring constantly, until the sauce is boiling and thickened.

4. Stir the cheese into the hot sauce. Add the nutmeg, seasoned salt and pepper. Stir until the cheese is melted. Add the broccoli. Stir. Cut the potatoes in half. Place on the plates. Fluff up the insides with the fork. Spoon about ¼ cup (60 mL) broccoli sauce over each potato half. Makes 8 stuffed potato halves.

Pictured on page 199.

A delicious way to make ordinary baked
potatoes special. Thick and creamy broccoli
sauce in every mouthful.

Left: Corn Doggies, page 105
Top Right: Broccoli-Sauced Potatoes, page 198

Measurement Tables

Throughout this book measurements are given in Conventional and Metric measures. The tables below provide a quick reference for the standard measures, weights, temperatures, and sizes.

Spoons

Conventional Measure	Metric Standard Measure Millilitre (mL)
1/8 teaspoon (tsp.)	0.5 mL
1/4 teaspoon (tsp.)	1 mL
1/2 teaspoon (tsp.)	2 mL
1 teaspoon (tsp.)	5 mL
2 teaspoons (tsp.)	10 mL
1 tablespoon (tbsp.)	15 mL

Cups

Conventional Measure	Metric Standard Measure Millilitre (mL)
1/4 cup (4 tbsp.)	60 mL
1/3 cup (5 tbsp.)	75 mL
1/2 cup (8 tbsp.)	125 mL
2/3 cup (10 tbsp.)	150 mL
3/4 cup (12 tbsp.)	175 mL
1 cup (16 tbsp.)	250 mL
4 cups	1000 mL(1 L)

Weights

Ounces (oz.)	Grams (g)
1 oz.	28 g
2 oz.	57 g
3 oz.	85 g
4 oz.	113 g
5 oz.	140 g
6 oz.	170 g
7 oz.	200 g
8 oz.	225 g
16 oz. (1 lb.)	454 g
32 oz. (2 lbs.)	900 g
35 oz. (2.2 lbs.)	1000 g (1 kg)

Oven Temperature

Fahrenheit (°F)	Celsius (°C)
175°	80°
200°	95°
225°	110°
250°	120°
275°	140°
300°	150°
325°	160°
350°	175°
375°	190°
400°	205°
425°	220°
450°	230°
475°	240°
500°	260°

Pans

Conventional Inches	Metric Centimetres
8×8 inch	20×20 cm
9×9 inch	22×22 cm
9×13 inch	22×33 cm
10×15 inch	25×38 cm
11×17 inch	28×43 cm
8×2 inch round	20×5 cm
9×2 inch round	22×5 cm
10×4 1/2 inch tube	25×11 cm
8×4×3 inch loaf	20×10×7.5 cm
9×5×3 inch loaf	22×12.5×7.5 cm

Casseroles

Conventional Quart (qt.)	Metric Litre (L)
1 qt.	1 L
1 1/2 qt.	1.5 L
2 qt.	2 L
2 1/2 qt.	2.5 L
3 qt.	3 L
4 qt.	4 L

Recipe Index

206 Recipe Index